THE
GROWTH
DEPARTMENT

"Everyone wants 10x growth, but most teams are stuck doing 2x work. Real compounding happens when you raise the floor. This is the playbook."

Dr. Benjamin Hardy, bestselling author of
10x Is Easier Than 2x and *The Science of Scaling*

THE
GROWTH
DEPARTMENT

HOW ACCOUNT MANAGEMENT AND CUSTOMER SUCCESS BECOME THE REVENUE ENGINE

ALEX RAYMOND

Published by AMplify Media.

Portions of this book are based on conversations from the *Account Management Secrets* podcast, produced by AmplifyAM, Inc.

AMplify™ and The AMplify Method™ are trademarks of AmplifyAM, Inc. Trademark applications are pending in the United States.

Cover design and interior design by Karolina Kruk-Umięcka.

Illustrations © 2026 AmplifyAM, Inc.

Hardcover ISBN: 979-8-9941685-1-6
Paperback ISBN: 979-8-9941685-0-9
Kindle ISBN: 979-8-9941685-2-3
EPUB ISBN: 979-8-9941685-3-0
iBook ISBN: 979-8-9941685-4-7

First edition, January 2026

ADVANCE PRAISE FOR
THE GROWTH DEPARTMENT

"Everyone wants 10x growth but most teams are stuck doing 2x work — chasing new logos while the base stays flat. Real compounding happens when you raise the floor: better retention, better expansion, better systems underneath. This book shows you how."

Dr. Benjamin Hardy, organizational psychologist and bestselling author of *10x Is Easier Than 2x* and *The Science of Scaling*

"The CCO job isn't just to make customers happy — it's also to make revenue predictable. That means surfacing risk early, building systems that scale, and earning the trust of the executive team one accurate forecast at a time. *The Growth Department* is the clearest articulation I've seen of what that actually takes."

Josh Abdulla, Chief Customer Officer, Asana

"I spent my career proving what Account Management can be. I grew one account from $50,000 to $10 million. I grew another by 25x. I hit quota 17 years straight. But I had no playbook, no system, no language to explain what I was doing or teach it to others. I built the method by trial and error, alone. This book is everything I figured out — and everything I wish someone had handed me when I started."

"An invaluable guide to the individual skills and organizational capabilities necessary to drive predictable customer expansion."

"Alex changed how I think about my accounts, my clients, and my career. This book is the whole system in one place."

"I've done over 3,000 customer interviews, and I've seen this every time: Your customers will tell you everything — if you ask the right questions and shut up long enough to hear the answer. Alex calls it Relentless Curiosity. I call it the difference between Account Managers who react and Account Managers who lead."

"Customer leaders lose credibility by reporting activities such as QBRs completed and health scores updated, instead of reporting outcomes. Activities don't matter to executives. What they care about is whether you can predict and deliver revenue outcomes accurately. *The Growth Department* finally gives Post-Sale teams the system to do that."

"Call it Customer Success and you'll be funded like support. Call it the Growth Department and you might actually get the investment it deserves. Alex makes the case — and backs it up with a system."

Rav Dhaliwal, Investor at Crane Venture Partners

"I've owned the customer relationship at the executive level—and I know how hard it is to justify investment without tying impact to growth. The Growth Department finally gives customer leaders the language, framework, and proof to show how their work drives revenue, not just satisfaction."

Mary Poppen, President & CXO, HRIZONS EX

"Imagine if every customer could walk away tomorrow. In that moment, accountability stops being a principle and becomes survival. Alex exposes the uncomfortable truth in this book: every business ultimately lives or dies by the customer value it delivers."

Anthony DeShazor, Founder, Protia Revenue Systems

"I've spent over 20 years in customer success watching the function struggle to be taken seriously. The problem isn't the people. It's the model. The Growth Department replaces the old model with one that earns us a seat at the revenue table. It's a must-read."

Chad Horenfeldt, Customer Success executive and author
of *The Strategic Customer Success Manager*

TABLE OF CONTENTS

Introduction: The $10 Million Question   11

Part I: The Post-Sale Tax   19
Chapter 1: Blind Spots Costing Millions   21
Chapter 2: The Irrefutable Economics of Expansion   35
Interlude: Are You Still Managing Accounts Like It's 1999?   51

Part II: The Growth Department   53
Chapter 3: You Are the Growth Department   55
Chapter 4: Value Before Revenue   69
Chapter 5: How Winning Teams Operate   83
Interlude: The Principles of the Growth Department   95

Part III: The AMplify Method   99
Chapter 6: Solve Bigger Problems   101
Chapter 7: Relentless Curiosity   113
Chapter 8: Act Like an Owner   125
Chapter 9: Protect Your Energy   135
Interlude: Bringing The AMplify Method to Your Team   147

Part IV: Running the Growth Department   149
Chapter 10: Building the Growth Department   151
Chapter 11: The Growth Operating System   161
Interlude: The 90-Day Growth Department Install Plan   171
Conclusion: You're in the Driver's Seat   175

Appendix A: The Growth Department Charter   179
Appendix B: The Internal Pitch Kit   183
Notes   187
Acknowledgements   190
About the Author   191

THE $10 MILLION QUESTION

"Where do you want to be in five years?"

Joanna Hagelberger, then an Account Manager at Vertafore, asked this question to a customer as they sat across from each other at a conference table. The client was a Top 5 health insurance company, and the account was worth about $50,000 a year. Not small, but not strategic. Just another account in her portfolio.

The customer sat back in their chair. It wasn't a hard question, but no vendor had ever asked it. Maybe not even their own leadership. Instead of answering right away, the customer said, "We'll have to get back to you."

Two weeks later, they came back with a deck that laid out where their business was heading and the risks and opportunities that lay ahead.

That conversation changed her posture. She showed up as a partner and asked: What would be different in five years? What would they need? What could they build together?

Over the years that followed, she grew that one account from $50,000 to $10 million in annual revenue. In the Account Management world, people celebrate 50% growth. Joanna delivered 200x.

Joanna isn't a unicorn. She didn't have a bigger budget or a better CRM. What made her extraordinary was *method*: the discipline to ask better questions, think in longer time horizons, and own the results she promised.

Most companies don't have a name for that work.

This book does: the Growth Department.

THE MISSING SYSTEM

Joanna worked at a normal company with normal tools and normal resources. So why aren't there more Joannas? Why do we celebrate 20% expansion like it's a win? Why don't we routinely hear of companies that expand customers by an order of magnitude or more?

Because most companies design Post-Sale to protect revenue, not create it.

Account Managers own most of the revenue but operate without the system to grow it. They're measured on retention but not equipped for expansion.

After the deal closes, the customer gets handed to the team responsible for renewals, expansion, and outcomes. That team works with outdated playbooks, if they have playbooks at all. They get a fraction of the investment Sales gets and none of the infrastructure.

I've watched companies overinvest in sales and marketing, watch profits erode, and still not understand why. They assume growth comes from net new logos. In modern B2B, that belief gets expensive fast. Real growth comes from customers who stay and expand. The companies that figure this out compound. The ones that don't keep pouring money into acquisition and wondering where the margin went.

I call this the Account Management Tax: the cost of running Post-Sale without a system. Preventable churn. Missed expansion. Unpredictable forecasts. Exhausted teams.

You know you're paying the tax when your best Account Manager leaves and three accounts go dark within 90 days because nobody else knows the relationships. A renewal you thought was solid turns into a negotiation because the champion left and you didn't know. Your CEO asks why NRR is flat and you can't point to a system, only to heroics that may or may not repeat next quarter.

Most Account Management teams aren't underperforming. They're under-positioned.

This book fixes that.

THE OLD PLAYBOOK IS DEAD

This book is not an upgrade to your current playbook. It's a replacement. If you try to install this inside the old model, you'll turn it into theater.

If your Post-Sale function talks about relationships instead of revenue, it gets funded like overhead. Measure activity instead of outcomes and you get cut when budgets tighten. Operate without a forecast and leadership treats you like a cost center.

The old model assumed retention was the default. It treated Customer Success as support with a nicer title. It let Account Management own most of the revenue while giving it a fraction of the investment. It confused being a "trusted advisor" with being "trusted to do whatever the customer asks."

That model is expensive, and it's dying.

The Old Playbook says "we're trusted advisors," but you advise while they decide. No commercial authority. It claims "we're customer-centric," but you measure activities, not outcomes. You track QBRs completed, not revenue retained. It insists "our customers love us," but love doesn't show up on a P&L. Your NPS is high and your NRR is flat.

This is the Old Playbook, the 1999 version of the job. Post-Sale is maintenance. The function gets funded like support. The team gets positioned as helpers instead of owners.

The Growth Department starts from a different premise: existing-customer revenue is not maintenance. It's the most profitable growth in the company, and it closes faster than anything Sales is chasing. The function that owns it should be funded and structured like a growth engine.

If any of this sounds familiar, you're not behind. You're normal. The Old Playbook is what most companies run because it's what they inherited. But just because you inherited it doesn't mean it's a strategy.

If you're still running Post-Sale like it's 1999, this book will make that uncomfortable. Good.

TEN YEARS OF THE SAME STORY

I started working with Account Management leaders about ten years ago. Everywhere I went, it was the same story.

The people in these roles knew they were creating value. They knew the function had more potential. And inside their own companies, nobody seemed to care.

I used to run events called KAMCon for Account Managers. Leaders would come up to me between sessions and say the same thing: "My team is responsible for so much revenue, and we have to fight to get budget just to attend a conference like this. I'm not even sure my CEO could describe what we do all day."

These were the people holding the company together. And nobody knew it.

I heard that hundreds of times. After a while, I stopped believing it was a motivation problem. It's a design problem.

I've spent the last decade trying to fix it. I co-founded Kapta, a software company built for Account Management teams. I host the *Account Management Secrets* podcast. I now run AMplify and spend my weeks with Post-Sale leaders trying to fix retention, expansion, and forecast accuracy (the "AM" is capitalized as an homage to the great work that Account Managers do around the world). Through Kapta and AMplify, I've worked with hundreds of companies and thousands of Account Managers across dozens of industries. I've seen what works and what doesn't.

What's missing: an operating system.

This book gives you one: a scoreboard, portfolio model, risk framework, playbook, and cadences that make the work predictable. It shows you how to make the work legible to the people who fund it.

IF THIS IS YOU

Throughout this book, I use "Account Manager" as a placeholder for anyone responsible for retention, expansion, and long-term customer outcomes. Your company might call it Account Management, Customer Success, Post-Sale, or Client Services. Whatever the title, the job is largely the same.

You lead Post-Sale. You got handed NRR, churn, and surprise renewals, and you're expected to fix it without authority or a map. Maybe you got promoted. Maybe you're stuck in internal politics and can't get traction. Maybe your best people are burning out and walking out the door.

Or you're an Account Manager who doesn't have the title but does the work anyway. You see the distance between what your function could be and how your company treats it. You want vocabulary and a system you can actually use.

This isn't Account Management 101, and it isn't a book for scaled Customer Success managing portfolios of 150 accounts. I'm not going to walk you through how to run a QBR. I'm assuming you already have experience, you're committed to the craft, and you're ready to think at the level of the function, not just the account.

What I am going to do is dismantle the old way of thinking and replace it with a map for what to build, vocabulary you can use with your team and executives, and proof that you're not alone in trying to change how this works.

THE MAP

The book is organized in four parts.

Part I lays the foundation. It makes the case for why the economics of growth have changed and why existing-customer revenue is where the real money is.

Part II builds the operating system. You will learn Keep, Grow, No Surprises and what it means to run your function as a Growth Department.

Part III introduces the AMplify Method. This is where you learn to create capacity and develop the commercial skills that make expansion natural instead of forced.

Part IV is about building the department. It covers how to lead, how to install the system inside your company, and how to make it stick.

You can read straight through or jump to the chapters that address your most pressing problems. Each chapter stands on its own, but the book builds a complete system.

A NOTE FOR EXECUTIVES

If you're a CEO, CRO, or CFO, this book is about a problem you own.

The problems described in these chapters aren't complaints. They're diagnostics. Your Post-Sale function is under-positioned. Not for lack of talent, but because nobody built it to do what you're now asking it to do.

Joanna generated $100 million in lifetime value from a single customer. She didn't have more resources than your team does. She had method. That potential exists inside your company right now: in your accounts, your people, and the customers waiting for someone to ask where they want to be in five years.

Joanna built her system. This book shows you how to build yours.

PART I

THE POST-SALE TAX

CHAPTER 1:

BLIND SPOTS COSTING MILLIONS

The team erupts in cheers. A sales rep has just closed a million-dollar deal, and the whole company knows about it. The gong echoes through the office, Slack fills with champagne emojis, and the CEO jumps in to add congratulations. At the next all-hands, the deal will be celebrated like a trophy. The rep is already packing for President's Club in Cancun.

Two years later, that same customer is at $3 million a year. It's one of your most profitable accounts.

But where is the celebration?

No gong. No champagne. No Cancun. The Account Manager who made it happen gets a pat on the back, maybe lunch with the boss, and then it's back to work.

I call this the Curse of the Unsung Hero. You deliver compounding value, the company celebrates the sale, and then it's on to the next deal.

The 1999 business model was built to win deals, not built to grow them.

In most B2B companies, Post-Sale teams manage 73% of annual revenue and nearly all of the profit. The economics of growth have changed, and companies that haven't caught up are paying for it in depressed valuations, burned-out talent, and growth that never compounds the way it should.

THE INVISIBLE BURDEN

If you lead Account Management, Customer Success, or any Post-Sale function, you already know this dynamic. Your team is the one that keeps customers when competitors are circling. They take the late-night call. They absorb the friction. They turn "we might churn" into "we're fine" without anyone else ever hearing about it.

That's the bind. When things go well, no one notices. When something breaks, everyone notices. Your best work leaves no evidence.

You own the number, but you don't control the inputs. You're accountable for renewals, expansion, and customer health while other teams decide what gets sold, what gets built, and what gets fixed. You inherit the consequences of decisions you didn't make.

Sales reps get a top-of-the-line tech stack and a clear number to hit. Your team gets a number too, but not the inputs to control it. Then leadership asks why forecasts are soft.

Sales is Batman. Account Management is Robin.

But look at the actual numbers and the mistake becomes obvious. Robin has the money. Most of the revenue is already in the building. The question is whether your company is structured to grow it.

FOLLOW THE MONEY

Want to know what the company really values? Don't read the mission statement. Follow the money.

Sales is 40-50% of go-to-market headcount and produces 27% of revenue. Post-Sale is a fraction of headcount and delivers 73% of total revenue every year.

The most profitable revenue in the company is managed by the least funded team in the building.

Tooling tells the same story: sales tech stacks run tens of thousands per rep. Account Managers and CS teams operate on a few thousands dollars per person, often sharing a CRM license built for sales workflows and never adapted for retention.

Training follows the pattern. New sales hires get weeks of onboarding, call coaching, and ramp time; new Account Managers get a book of business and a login.

Same with executive attention. Pipeline reviews happen every week and are regularly attended by the C-suite; account reviews happen when something gets escalated.

Sales kickoff gets a keynote. Post-Sale sits in the back row and gets told to be "more strategic."

A 2025 Gartner survey of 243 CSOs found that 73% are prioritizing growth from existing customers, and 57% see account retention and growth as a top-3 priority. But the same survey identified what Gartner calls the "customer value disconnect": suppliers struggle to convert the promise of their value proposition into realized customer value. As Gartner's Daniel Hawkyard put it, "Customers are not just buying a product; they are buying the promise of value realization."

That's the polite research term for what you already feel day to day: customers don't experience the value you think you're delivering.

That disconnect is the Account Management Tax by another name.

The org chart was built when new logos were the only growth that mattered. So were the investing decisions, the resource allocation, the comp plans, the career paths, the board metrics. All of it was designed for acquisition. That structure is still in place.

And still, the customer stays. Which is exactly why the blind spot survives.

THE WORK NO ONE SEES

You didn't end up in this work by accident. People who thrive in Account Management share something: they see the whole picture when everyone else sees only their piece.

Sales sees the deal, Product sees the roadmap, Finance sees the numbers. You see how all of it connects inside a real customer's world, and you see what happens when the pieces don't fit.

What looks like improvisation from the outside is actually expertise. You hold a dozen dependencies in your head at once: bridging sales promises with product reality, managing your customer's evolving goals and internal politics, tracking the exec sponsor who just left and the new one who doesn't know you yet. Most people in your company see only their slice. You see the entire machine.

You know these moments. Nobody else in your company does:

→ You walked in prepared for a QBR that took days to organize, only to sit alone because the customer ghosted you.

→ You inherited a portfolio and saw within minutes that an account was mis-sold, even though the rest of the company celebrates it as healthy.

→ You discovered a critical internal error and contained it immediately, knowing that exposing the mistake would create unnecessary risk for the customer relationship.

→ You sat in the back of a sales training, if you were invited at all, translating on the fly because none of the content was built for the work you actually do.

These moments decide retention and expansion long before the renewal conversation starts. This is the gray zone where revenue stability is won or lost, in moments the company never tracks and rarely celebrates.

I've reviewed hundreds of account plans and QBR decks. The pattern is always the same: the Account Manager sees the whole picture, and nobody else realizes how much is being held together by one person.

Now imagine what this talent could do with an actual system behind it.

Craig Rosenberg co-founded TOPO, the go-to-market research firm acquired by Gartner in 2020, where he became a Distinguished VP Analyst. He now serves as Chief Platform Officer at Scale Venture Partners. When I asked him about the skill difference between Sales and Post-Sale teams, his observation surprised me.

"Good Customer Success people and good Account Management people are better at identifying business value than the new-logo seller," he said. "It's nuts."

The people closest to the customer understand value best. They just don't have the structure to prove it or the authority to scale it.

Joanna Hagelberger is one of those people. You met her in the introduction, the Account Manager who turned a $50,000 account into a $10 million partnership. What I didn't tell you is what she walked into when she joined Vertafore: there was no Account Management function, no CRM, and the Salesforce contract was signed the week before she started.

Over the next 17 years, she exceeded quota every single year. She didn't do it by working harder. She did it by changing what the customer saw as valuable and making it measurable. We'll return to it.

THE OWNERSHIP VOID

If I asked your CEO who owns growth from existing customers, could they answer in one sentence?

Most can't. The company was never built with an answer.

Sales assumes you run Quarterly Business Reviews (QBRs) and keep customers warm until the next expansion opportunity. Product treats you as a conduit for feature requests. Support sees you as an escalation path for their hardest tickets. Finance thinks you negotiate renewals. And somewhere in the C-suite, someone still believes Customer Success shouldn't touch revenue because it might compromise the relationship.

Anthony Iannarino is one of the most respected voices in B2B sales, the author of books like *The Only Sales Guide You'll Ever Need*, and *Elite Sales Strategies*. On the *Account Management Secrets* podcast, he told me about one of his clients, an Account Management team that lost a $5 million customer. Not to a competitor. Not because of pricing. The relationship faded away, because no one was accountable for leading it.

"They were not doing what they were supposed to be doing," he said. "If they would have taken the lead and said, we're going to help you through this thing, they would have been fine."

That's $5 million in annual revenue, lost to neglect.

"You already have the two things you need," he said. "Contracts and contacts. Why would you go get somebody brand new when you're not growing the clients you have now?"

That's what happens when nobody owns growth after the sale.

HEROICS MASK BROKEN SYSTEMS

Here's what happens when you don't have a system in Post-Sale: your best people become the system.

They catch the mistake before it reaches the customer. They stay late to fix what shouldn't have broken. They run the extra meeting, write the follow-up, smooth over the handoff, and keep the account calm.

And that work produces a dangerous outcome: nothing looks broken.

The customer doesn't escalate. The renewal still closes. The quarter still lands. So leadership learns the wrong lesson. They don't learn, "we got lucky." They learn, "we're fine."

That's why heroic acts are so expensive. Not because they don't work, but because they work too well. They erase the evidence that would have forced the organization to change.

This is the part nobody wants to hear: your heroics are keeping the system broken.

Every time you fix a problem that should have surfaced, you train others inside your company to ignore it. The late nights, the saves, the "I'll just handle it" moments don't get filed as risk. They get filed as competence.

So you get thanked, and nothing gets fixed.

Heroics don't prove you're strong. They prove the system is weak.

And heroics aren't free. You pay in nights and weekends, in the slow burn of being the person who always cleans it up, and socially too. The more you compensate for broken systems, the more you interrupt other teams to do it: pulling Product into exceptions, Sales into cleanup, Services into favors. Even when you're right, you become the person who "always has an issue."

Meanwhile leadership sees the customer still renewing and assumes the machine is working. They don't see the midnight oil, the internal resentment, or what it costs to hold it all together.

So the company keeps underfunding the function. Your team keeps absorbing the problems. And when it finally breaks in a way you can't contain, leadership calls it "a retention problem."

It wasn't. It was a design problem.

CCO: A TITLE WITHOUT A CHECKBOOK

Many companies have tried to solve the ownership problem by creating a Chief Customer Officer. Put someone in the C-suite who wakes up every day thinking about existing customers.

I've interviewed dozens of CCOs on my podcast. I know these people. They're talented, experienced leaders who understand exactly what needs to happen. They see the whole picture. They know where the value is leaking. They know what it would take to fix it.

They just can't get anyone to fund it.

Mary Poppen, co-founder, president and CXO of HRIZONS EX and former CCO at LinkedIn and SAP, has managed over $1 billion in recurring revenue across multiple CCO roles. When I asked her to describe the job of the CCO, she said: "I am responsible for making sure that our customers are getting value and that they want to continue the partnership forever."

Poppen sees two things as non-negotiable: delivering the value you promised, and doing so as a trusted partner. If either is missing, customers start referring to you as a "vendor." And in her experience, when you become a vendor, you've already lost the customer. You just don't know it yet.

Then she told me what it takes. "It requires resources. It requires budget. It requires systems, processes, and people to get it done."

The organization wants "forever." But it won't fund what it takes to earn it.

The CRO gets the number and the budget follows. The CCO gets the title without the checkbook.

So you get executives with a decade of customer experience, real insight into what drives retention, and a genuine vision for how the company could grow, and you watch them spend their days begging other departments for resources.

The title shows intent. The budget shows ownership.

Leadership sometimes tries to fix this by splitting the number. One CCO I spoke with described splitting revenue accountability with the Chief Revenue Officer. It was meant to encourage alignment, but it created the opposite. When two executives share the same number, neither truly owns it. Incentives blur, priorities conflict, and the customer ends up navigating a divided organization.

Rod Cherkas, author of *The Chief Customer Officer Playbook* and *REACH*, has watched this pattern repeat. "If you don't optimize for retention, expansion, and profitability, you're not in the growth business. You're in the coordination business."

You want to know why Post-Sale stays broken? Because we keep putting our best people in roles designed to fail, and then we wonder why nothing changes.

WHAT THIS IS COSTING YOU

Missed expansion. Your team is so buried in retention fires that they never get around to growing accounts. Customers who would have bought more never get asked, because no one had the time or the authority to ask them.

Renewal risk disguised as wins. Sometimes a customer renews even when things went badly, and leadership calls it a win. Luck is not a system. The next renewal might not survive the same friction.

Knowledge attrition. Your best Account Managers hold years of customer knowledge in their heads: relationships, history, context that lives nowhere else. If the role stays thankless and under-resourced, you increase the odds your best people leave. When they do, that knowledge walks out with them. Replacing it takes months. Some of it never comes back.

Forecast credibility. Net Revenue Retention has become the metric boards use to judge leadership quality. A CRO who can't explain why NRR is flat or declining is a CRO on borrowed time. Boards don't ask for stories. They ask for a forecast they can trust. The pressure rolls downhill, but the problem lives upstream.

I described the situation in the introduction as the Account Management Tax: the compound cost of running a growth function with a maintenance mindset. None of this shows up as one big failure. It shows up as drag. A little slower every quarter. A little harder to hit the number.

Those costs aren't random. You designed them in.

SIGNS YOU'RE RUNNING ON HEROICS

If you recognize your team in this list, you are not alone.

→ Your team jumps in to rescue situations that should never have reached them.

→ You praise scrappiness even though it means every issue takes longer to solve than it should.

→ Your people with the most potential avoid visibility because speaking up rarely changes anything.

→ Your team does the work while other functions get the budget, the tools, and the airtime.

→ You sit through kickoffs and trainings built for other teams and translate them on the fly.

→ You make do with minimal resources while the highest-margin revenue in the company sits under your care.

And if you're an executive reading this list and recognizing your company, the problem isn't your people. It's the system you built around them.

CHAPTER 2:

THE IRREFUTABLE ECONOMICS OF EXPANSION

I have never been to your executive meeting, but I know the agenda: a parade of pipeline updates, a detailed review of stalled deals, week-by-week forecasts of new logos, pressure to commit the number, and a room full of stressed leaders trying to deliver growth.

And then? Fifteen minutes for existing customers, if time allows. More often, the conversation gets pushed to a sidebar. 90% of the meeting goes to the part of the business that burns cash. Almost nothing goes to the part that creates it.

Your meeting agenda mirrors your growth strategy, and that strategy is backwards. You're chasing top-line revenue while ignoring profitable growth. You're missing the single greatest driver of growth, profitability, and valuation: Net Revenue Retention.

This is how most companies grew up. Acquisition built the business. Expansion funds it now. But the meeting agenda never caught up.

New customers matter. Most are unprofitable in year one. Everyone in that conference room understands the resource lift required to land them: months of marketing spend, costly sales effort, evaluation cycles that stretch over quarters, legal reviews that slow everything down, painful price concessions to close the deal, and the onboarding work that pulls resources from every corner of the company.

Let's start with the cost of getting customers in the door.

ACQUISITION IS AN INVESTMENT AT RISK

When you acquire a new customer, you're actually paying for them. Real dollars, out the door, before you see a cent back. Marketing spend, sales salaries, conference booths, onboarding hours, implementation resources. That's cash you've spent on a customer who hasn't paid you back.

How much cash? Acquiring $1 of new revenue costs about $1.18. You spend more than you get.

Until the payback period ends, every customer is an investment at risk.

And you won't break even for a while. Benchmarks put CAC payback at 20 to 30 months, longer in enterprise. Until a customer crosses that line, your acquisition spend is a bet that hasn't paid off yet.

Now think about what happens when that customer churns in year one.

Every dollar you spent to acquire them is gone. Incinerated. And you have to spend it all over again just to replace them. You don't miss the upside. You pay the full cost twice.

If you let a customer walk before they hit the payback threshold, you didn't lose revenue. You destroyed capital. You paid for a customer who never paid you back.

As Account Management and Customer Success, your objective is to get accounts across the profitability line. Every account you save in year one is capital you didn't destroy. Every account that makes it to year two is an investment that finally started paying back.

That's not support work. That's protecting the money the company already spent.

PROFIT COMES AFTER THE FIRST RENEWAL

Once a customer clears the payback period, they become profitable. Renewal revenue hits the books without the upfront costs of a new sale.

Expansion revenue is more profitable still. Selling into an existing account takes a fraction of the time, cost, and effort. The buying structure is already in place. Stakeholders know your team. You have results to point to.

Remember that $1.18 it costs to acquire a dollar of new revenue? Expanding an existing customer costs about $0.28. Renewing them costs $0.13.

A dollar of expansion is four times more efficient than a dollar of acquisition.

When the sales team rings the gong for a $100,000 deal, the company hasn't made $100,000. It has spent $118,000 to acquire a contract that won't break even for two years. When an Account Manager expands a customer by $100,000, the company keeps most of it. No parade. No Cancun.

Acquisition burns cash. Retention and expansion deliver it back. This is where Account Management earns its place: not as support, but as the team responsible for the most efficient growth in the company.

THE GROWTH HIDING IN PLAIN SIGHT

Account Management is the team that turns "land" into "expand." You nurture a small account until it becomes a major relationship, and because you understand the customer's goals as deeply as your own, you see opportunities others miss.

Ebsta analyzed more than 650,000 opportunities across nearly 400 companies and found that 52% of net new revenue came from existing customers.

Hang on, what?

Not renewals. Not contracted increases. Net new dollars, the same kind of growth your company celebrates as "new business." Guy Rubin, Founder of Ebsta, confirmed: "52% of additional revenue our organizations generated last year didn't come from new logos. It came from our existing customers."

The same study showed why. Expansion deals close in 52 days versus 91 for new business. Win rates hit 45% versus 18%. And you need five stakeholders instead of eight. Lower cost. Higher win rates. Shorter cycles. Simpler deals. That's the growth hiding in plain sight.

So why do dashboards still treat it like an afterthought?

Joanna Hagelberger's 200x expansion of a single account, the equivalent of dozens of new logo wins, was achieved by one person inside one relationship. That's what happens when you invest in the accounts you already have.

Yet dashboards and board decks still fixate on new logos. CFOs tend to see the full picture because they track payback and gross margin closely. Many CEOs and CROs still equate growth with acquisition. That's where attention flows, so that's where resources follow.

There's one assumption that keeps this misunderstanding locked in place.

THE FALLACY OF RECURRING REVENUE

One of the most dangerous illusions in modern business is the myth of "recurring revenue."

It shows up everywhere: Monthly Recurring Revenue, Annual Recurring Revenue, renewal forecasts. Leaders love these metrics because they suggest stability. Recurring revenue sounds automatic, like rent checks appearing on the first of the month.

But recurring revenue is a fallacy. I've watched companies lose major accounts they considered "locked in" simply because someone stopped paying attention.

There is no such thing as recurring revenue. There is only re-earned revenue.

Every dollar must be re-earned. Today, customers have more information, greater leverage, and lower switching costs than ever before. Every contract faces deep scrutiny, renewals included. One quarter of missed value can undo years of goodwill.

So why does the illusion persist? Because the optics are convenient. Predictable revenue smooths choppy forecasts. It reassures boards and allows leaders to talk about "annuities" and guaranteed growth.

But the reality underneath is fragile. Revenue becomes instantly vulnerable the moment the company treats it as guaranteed. When leaders assume renewals are automatic, the work required to earn them slips down the priority list, and that neglect shows up as inevitable churn.

Because revenue isn't actually recurring, your mindset can't be passive.

ACTIVE RETENTION: EARN EVERY RENEWAL

The best Account Managers I know operate with a healthy sense of paranoia. They assume every renewal is at risk, that competitors have already made the call. They act like every account is being re-evaluated in the background, because it usually is.

These aren't the "no news is good news" folks who passively wait for contracts to expire. They understand that keeping and growing an account takes the same intensity as winning it in the first place.

Passive renewal management assumes revenue continues unless something breaks. Active Retention assumes the customer always has a choice.

> **Active Retention is the mindset that revenue is earned, not recurring.**

Sales teams live by process: pipelines, stages, forecasts, inspection calls, structured reviews. Your retention work demands the same discipline. If growth depends on renewals and expansions, then renewals deserve their own dedicated forecast, cadence, and scorecard.

Every Account Manager should be able to answer three questions at any moment:

→ Which renewals are secure, and why.

→ Which are at risk, and what is causing it.

→ What the recovery plan and timeline are.

Professionals know the exact state of their accounts and can explain how they are managing risk. Part II will show how to operationalize this discipline.

NRR: THE SCOREBOARD

Net Revenue Retention measures what happens to revenue from the same customers over time. It rolls expansion, churn, and contraction into a single number that tells you whether your customer base is growing or shrinking.

$$NRR = \frac{\text{Starting Revenue + Expansion Revenue – Churned Revenue}}{\text{Starting Revenue}} \times 100$$

Start with revenue from a cohort of customers. Add expansion. Subtract churn and contraction. Divide by where you started. No new logos enter the calculation. NRR only counts what happened with the customers you already had.

At 100%, your base holds steady. At 110%, your base grows before you add a single new customer. At 95%, your base leaks, and you're forced to replace the loss at full acquisition cost before any real growth begins.

When NRR falls below 100%, your revenue is shrinking, not growing. Imagine you start with $100 million. At 95% NRR, you begin next year at $95 million before anyone sells a thing. You're in a hole. That $5 million has to be replaced at full acquisition cost just to return to flat. To grow 20%, you now need $25 million in new business, starting with $5 million to refill the leak. When your base shrinks, urgency skyrockets. NRR is not a Customer Success metric. It is a leadership metric.

NRR is not a Customer Success metric. It is a leadership metric.

Now picture the same company with 110% NRR. You start the year at $110 million. You're already growing before you add a single new logo.

A company stuck at 95% spends its life running uphill. A company at 110% builds momentum year after year.

Picture a $100 million business that adds $20 million in net new revenue every year. After three years, the difference is dramatic. At 95% NRR, you land at $142.8 million. You're growing, but recovering that lost revenue is a perennial tax. At 110% NRR, you land at $199.3 million. Same sales effort. Completely different outcome.

NRR is the scoreboard. Not pipeline. Not bookings. Not Net Promoter Score® (NPS).

A note on Gross Revenue Retention: GRR answers a simpler question. If you sold nothing extra, how much of the base did you actually keep? The formula removes expansion from the equation. GRR tells you how leaky the base is. NRR shows compounding growth. GRR shows how hard you're working just to stand still.

THINK LIKE A PORTFOLIO MANAGER

If NRR is the scoreboard, your customer base is the portfolio producing the return.

Portfolios follow a power law. Some accounts will grow. Some will stay flat. Some will churn. You won't save them all. Budget cuts, acquisitions, leadership changes: some attrition is baked into the base before you ever touch it.

Here's the part most people don't want to hear: the flat accounts are the majority. Most of your book will stay flat. That's not failure. That's the shape of the distribution.

So where does growth come from? A small number of accounts. If you're running a 3-5% expansion rate across your book, and you have a hundred accounts, that means three to five of them are actually going to grow. Three to five.

Now ask yourself: what's the opportunity cost of focusing on the wrong ones?

The math is getting more extreme. Frank Cespedes is a Senior Lecturer at Harvard Business School and the author of *Sales Management That Works*. He told me, "We've always had the 80-20 rule, but that's now closer to 90-10."

When the right account expands, it changes the year. But it's also the risk. As Cespedes put it: "You can't lose a lot of money with small customers. It's with big customers where you really test the validity of a value proposition and your business strategy."

Not every account is a growth account. The skill is knowing which ones are.

WHY INVESTORS OBSESS OVER NRR

Investors will forgive a lot. They won't forgive a leaky base. NRR is the signal that tells them whether a company's growth is durable or built on sand.

When NRR falls below 100%, new business must constantly replace the loss. When NRR rises above 100%, the customer base fuels its own growth. Investors will only accept the second scenario.

This obsession intensifies in volatile markets. Expansion revenue is faster, cheaper, and far steadier than anything derived from net new acquisition. High NRR means customers are getting value and voting with their wallets. Low NRR means something is broken.

Companies with NRR above 120% trade at valuation multiples more than 60% higher than the median. Each one-point lift in NRR increases enterprise value by 12-18% over five years.

Craig Rosenberg captured the board-level view on my podcast: "Boards care about retention and expansion because those metrics tell them the most about durability." Durable companies generate predictable, profitable growth.

NRR has become shorthand for assessing leadership quality. Strong NRR reflects clear priorities, aligned teams, and reliable value delivery. Weak NRR reveals operational confusion and waste.

That's why investors dissect cohort curves, expansion ratios, and renewal patterns during diligence. They don't ask for your story. They ask for the cohort curve.

For Account Managers, the takeaway is simple: investors no longer bet on acquisition activity. They bet on expansion efficiency.

YOU CAN'T IGNORE THE ECONOMICS

Acquisition burns cash. Retention and expansion generate it. NRR is the clearest measure of whether your growth model works.

If any of this surprised you, you're not alone. Most people in Post-Sale roles have never seen these numbers laid out clearly. They know their work matters, but they've never had the language to explain why. Now you do.

What does this mean on Monday morning? It means you stop treating renewal as paperwork and start treating it as pipeline. It means you walk into budget conversations with math, not stories.

Understanding this isn't optional. As you build your career, your ability to speak the language of capital efficiency, retention economics, and enterprise value will determine whether you're treated as overhead or recognized as a growth engine. The people who understand these dynamics get funded. The people who don't get cut.

Every problem in this chapter traces back to the Old Playbook. Forecast uncertainty? It never gave Post-Sale a number to own. Fire drills at quarter-end? Renewals were paperwork, not pipeline.

Surprise churn? No risk system, because retention was assumed. Burnout disguised as dedication? People owned revenue without the authority to control it.

In Part I we named the problem and proved the economics. Part II will show you what to do about it.

You're not a support function waiting for recognition. You're at the heart of your company's growth. The next section will show you how to operate like it: how to position yourself as the Growth Department, how to focus your time on what drives the number. And how to build durable, compounding growth.

THE CAPITAL REALLOCATION TEST

Every budget cycle, your company decides where to put money, effort, and people. Headcount. Tooling. Initiatives. Bets.

Run the Capital Reallocation Test: is that dollar chasing a customer you don't have yet, or growing one you already won?

Most companies keep feeding the expensive dollar and starving the efficient one. Then they wonder why growth gets harder every year.

Walk into the CFO meeting ready to make it concrete.

Start with the risk window. "Our CAC payback is roughly 20 to 30 months. Until we're past that, every new customer is an investment at risk. If we churn early, that's not lost revenue. It's destroyed capital."

Name the profit curve. "Most of the profit shows up after the first renewal. Acquisition burns cash. Renewal and expansion return margin. That's why NRR is the real scoreboard."

Put the math on the table. "It costs about $1.18 to acquire a dollar of new revenue. Roughly $0.28 to expand. And $0.13 to renew. We're funding the least efficient dollar."

Make a specific ask. "I want a two-quarter pilot: reallocate 5% of acquisition budget into Post-Sale capacity focused on renewals and expansion. We'll run a weekly renewal risk forecast and review progress together."

Then ask:

→ What percentage of net new revenue came from existing customers last year?

→ What are our NRR and GRR trends over the last four quarters?

→ Where is churn happening relative to payback?

→ What would a five-point improvement in NRR do to valuation?

ARE YOU STILL MANAGING ACCOUNTS LIKE IT'S 1999?

So many Account Management teams are stuck using playbooks and mindsets from the previous century. Back in the day, customers were stickier. Switching costs were real and the competition was slower. If you landed the deal and didn't destroy the relationship, you kept the business.

That world is gone, and it's not coming back.

The old model assumed retention was the default. The new model recognizes that every customer is choosing you again, every quarter, whether there's a contract renewal or not.

Old Model	New Model
QBR as formality	QBR as strategic conversation
Activity tracked	Outcomes earned
Reactive support	Proactive account leadership
Heroics	Systems
Customer happiness	Customer results
"Recurring" revenue	Revenue re-earned
Fragmented ownership	One revenue system
Unsung Hero	The Growth Department

Look at each row. Where is your team right now? Where does it need to be?

Part II gives you the model that gets you there.

PART II

THE GROWTH DEPARTMENT

CHAPTER 3:

YOU ARE THE GROWTH DEPARTMENT

Look at your portfolio and add up the revenue. Now imagine all of it disappeared tomorrow.

The company's entire NRR number would collapse. New sales couldn't replace it fast enough. Marketing couldn't generate enough pipeline. The business depends on that revenue showing up. You're the one making sure it does.

That's not a support function. That's the foundation of durable growth.

Your company may not see it that way yet. Your title probably says Account Manager or Customer Success Manager. You report to someone who files your work under "retention." You see the ownership vacuum and assume that's just how it works.

That's the 1999 version of this job.

Part I made the economics clear: expansion beats acquisition, and most profit shows up after the first deal. The invisible burden, the heroics masking broken systems, the CCO without a checkbook. The function has no name.

When you call yourself Account Management, you sound like administration. When you call yourself Customer Success, you sound like support. Neither tells the CFO what you produce. So leadership funds you like overhead. When budgets tighten, you show up as a cost to cut instead of a system to protect.

Talk like a support function, get a support budget. Talk like a growth function, get treated like what you are: the engine of profitable revenue.

THE GROWTH DEPARTMENT

That's what I'm calling this work: The Growth Department.

Not the team running product experiments or optimizing marketing funnels. The function responsible for existing-customer revenue: renewals, expansion, and the relationships that determine whether the business compounds or stalls.

> **You are the Growth Department, whether your company calls it that or not.**

This isn't a reorg. It's a change in how you run the business after the sale.

Call it the right thing and leadership finally knows what to fund, and what to measure.

WHAT WINNING REALLY MEANS

Let's be clear about what this isn't: support, customer happiness, or QBR theater.

The Growth Department exists to help your company win.

Not to manage accounts. Not to check boxes. To drive the number.

Fred Kofman has advised executives at LinkedIn, Google, and Microsoft and has written several books on leadership, including *The Meaning Revolution*. He uses the analogy of a soccer team to show what happens when people confuse their tasks with their job.

He asks: "What is a defender's job on a soccer team?"

Most answer, "To stop the other team from scoring."

Kofman pushes further: "What's the job of the entire team?"

"To win."

So what is the real job of the defender? To help the team win. The same is true of the goalkeeper, the midfielders, and the forwards.

As Kofman says, "What's the primary job of every person in a company? To help the team win."

Winning is the test that keeps "Growth Department" from becoming another vague label. The danger is that you can look incredibly helpful and still lose at renewal.

That's why being "helpful" isn't a strategy. It's how you get stuck.

THE HELPFULNESS TRAP

Chad Horenfeldt has led customer teams for more than 20 years, including roles at Oracle and Meta. His book, *The Strategic Customer Success Manager*, argues that the days of reactive, support-focused Customer Success Managers are over. He learned why the hard way.

At a user group in Austin, the customers actually stood up and gave him a standing ovation. It felt like confirmation he was doing everything right. Then competition arrived, and he started to see his company losing customers. His conclusion: "Being helpful was really just not enough."

The standing ovation didn't matter when renewal time came.

In his book, he names four default modes: Firefighter, Entertainer, Fixer, Waiter. The Firefighter chases urgency, the Entertainer chases rapport, the Fixer chases answers, and the Waiter chases direction. All four of these modes make you feel productive, but none put you in the driver's seat.

As Horenfeldt puts it, "These traits work. And that's the trap."

These behaviors used to be enough. Companies could afford teams focused on making customers happy when capital was cheap and growth felt automatic. "Empathy without economics has become a liability," Horenfeldt says. "Non-strategic Customer Success Managers won't make it."

You can be loved and still get fired when the account leaves. Your customer can adore you and still cancel because the business case didn't survive budget season.

Keep, Grow, No Surprises is how you stop being helpful on principle and start being useful on purpose.

KEEP, GROW, NO SURPRISES

Your job is to help your company win. That means delivering profitable revenue back to the business.

How? Three ways.

You keep the customers you have. You grow the ones with potential. And you make sure leadership is never blindsided.

Keep. Grow. No Surprises.

KEEP   **GROW**   **NO SURPRISES**

That's the job. If an activity doesn't connect to one of these three, why is it on your calendar?

There's another reason the stakes are higher now, and it's uncomfortable to say out loud. Sales teams are less efficient than they used to be. Ebsta's findings are brutal: 78% of sellers missed quota last year. Win rates fell another 10%.

When new business acquisition is inefficient and unreliable, the company leans harder on the base. That means more pressure on Account Managers to hold the number. And when you lose an account, you don't just lose revenue. You blow a hole in the plan. There isn't a flood of new logos coming to cover the miss.

Keep

The first job of the Growth Department is to keep the customers you already have.

New business is getting harder. Quotas are down and most sellers still miss their number. That's why the opportunity sits with you. Your work steadies the revenue line when acquisition slows. Each renewal turns sunk cost into profit. Every extra year compounds margin and enterprise value.

Every renewal is a decision your customer makes again. The renewal isn't decided in the renewal call. It's decided on a random Tuesday when something breaks. Your response teaches them whether you're essential or replaceable.

A saved renewal is revenue you don't have to re-buy. That's what it means to keep.

Grow

"Land and expand" isn't only for technology companies. Nearly every business earns more revenue over time than at the start of a contract.

But reliable growth doesn't happen by accident. You're not sitting around waiting for opportunities to appear. You're doing the work that makes it possible: tracking results, staying close to your customer's priorities, framing new ways to create value before they ask.

Grow happens when you show up as the partner, not the helper. Customers expand with the person who can name the next problem before they do. The best expansion conversations don't start with your pitch. They start with the customer saying "We've been thinking about..." and you already know what's coming because you've been watching their business, not just your contract.

That's the difference between the Account Manager who hears "we're expanding to Europe" and scrambles to build a proposal, and the one who already sent a note three weeks ago saying "I noticed your job postings in London. Here's what we've seen work in regional rollouts."

No Surprises

You know the email. It thanks you for everything, praises your team, wishes you well, and then tells you they're not renewing.

Nothing stings like a customer leaving without warning, especially when your boss asks why you didn't see it coming. And if you've had that happen, you know how brutal it is. Not because you lost the account. Because you're about to sit in a room where someone asks, "How did we not know?" And the honest answer is: you didn't have a system for knowing.

The third job of the Growth Department is to make the business predictable.

Bad news isn't the problem. Surprises are. Customers will merge. Budgets will shrink. Priorities will change. None of that is in your control. But if you see it coming, you and the company can prepare. If you don't, the bad news gets worse.

Positive surprises aren't the goal either. When a customer suddenly triples their spend, it feels great, but it tells everyone you didn't have visibility into the account. Your company can't plan staffing, resources, or delivery around surprises, good or bad.

No Surprises means you forecast accurately, surface risks early, and communicate clearly. Leadership can plan with confidence.

WHAT THE GROWTH DEPARTMENT REFUSES TO OWN

The Growth Department owns Keep, Grow, No Surprises. It doesn't own everything else.

Boundaries are what separate a revenue function from a catch-all.

→ Reactive support tickets disguised as "relationship management." If it's a product issue, it goes to Support. If it's a service failure, it goes to Delivery. The Growth Department coordinates, but it doesn't absorb.

→ Unlimited customization requests that erode margins. Saying yes to everything isn't customer-centricity. It's margin destruction. Growth protects profitability, not just happiness.

→ Surprise escalations caused by upstream neglect. If Sales mis-sold the account, if Implementation dropped the ball, if Product shipped a breaking change, Growth shouldn't take the blame. It coordinates the fix and protects the customer, but it doesn't become the dumping ground.

→ Outcomes for customers who were never a fit. This is not about blame. It is about aligning accountability with control. Growth owns retention and expansion. It cannot own the fallout from structurally bad-fit deals. When a customer is not a fit, Growth manages the renewal decision professionally. The organization owns learning why the deal closed in the first place.

When the boundaries blur, so does the budget. When accountability is clear, investment follows.

THE GROWTH DEPARTMENT CONTRACT

If you want these outcomes from the Growth Department, you must grant these authorities.

→ You want No Surprises. That requires tolerance for early bad news. You hear about problems in Q1, not Q4.

→ Accurate forecasts only happen when Growth owns the number. Not Sales. Not Finance. Split the ownership, split the accountability.

→ Expansion needs commercial authority. Growth initiates those conversations. It doesn't wait for Sales to hand them off.

→ If you want churn down, fund the team that prevents it. Headcount ratios matter.

→ Predictable renewals require sequencing rights. Growth decides when outreach begins and owns the timeline.

The Growth Department delivers profitable revenue. But it can only deliver what it's authorized to own.

YOUR CALENDAR IS YOUR STRATEGY

Look at your calendar for next week. Every meeting, every review, every "quick sync."

Ask three questions: Does this help me keep a customer? Does it help me grow an account? Does it reduce the chance of a surprise?

If the answer is no, it's noise. And noise is where your authority leaks out.

You don't keep noise on your calendar because you're careless. You keep it because saying no feels political, because the loudest request wins, because you're trying to be a good teammate. That's how you lose your week. But the number doesn't care how helpful you were internally. The number only cares what happened with customers.

The Growth Department charter comes with decision rights. You decide which accounts get attention, where time goes, and which meetings die on the spot.

Nobody is going to hand you that authority. You take it by making choices and defending them.

That's what it means to run a portfolio. A portfolio has a strategy. Some accounts anchor stability. Some hold real upside. Some are costing you more than they're worth. When you see your book that way, the calendar stops being a schedule and starts being a resource allocation.

Every customer conversation is a retention moment. Every account plan is a growth decision. Every internal review is where you surface risk early instead of explaining it later.

Here's the test. Open your calendar for next week and tag every commitment: K for Keep, G for Grow, N for No Surprises, or X for none of the above. If more than a third of your time is tagged X, you're not running a portfolio. You're being run by one.

Chapter 9 turns this into a weekly rhythm.

THE GROWTH DEPARTMENT IN ACTION

David Karp has spent more than 30 years in Post-Sale leadership. He came up through Account Management and learned how to make the function impossible to ignore.

When he stepped into executive leadership, he stopped talking about "my team versus your team" and started talking about the company.

"I was able to quickly start to connect dots across teams," he said, "to say we're actually aiming for something bigger, which is value for the whole company."

That meant getting sales, product, and finance aligned around shared goals. Not because collaboration sounds nice, but because customers don't care about your org chart.

He built his team around an NRR target of 115%. He segmented accounts by growth potential, partnered closely with the CRO instead of competing for territory, and framed the function's purpose in language the whole company could understand: "The most important thing we do is help us keep the promises we make," he said. "Who has to make sure that happens? The Account Manager."

The results changed how other departments talked about the work. When DISQO rolled out a new set of company values, Karp expected to be the one presenting "championing the customer." Instead, the Chief Product Officer did it, using language Karp's team had been using for years.

That's the Growth Department operating at scale. Not a rebranding exercise. Not a turf war. A function that helps the company win and gets recognized for it.

When you operate as the Growth Department, other functions realign around you. Sales stops treating you as a handoff. Product starts asking what customers really need. Finance sees you as a revenue driver, not a cost center.

You're not asking for a seat at the table. You're pointing to the revenue that built the table.

Karp didn't transform his function by announcing a new name. He changed what his team believed they were there to deliver, and how they proved it every week. He didn't win influence by asking for it. He won it by showing the company the number, and building the rhythm to hit it.

"Growth Department" isn't a label you claim. It's a standard you rise to.

Operate like the Growth Department long enough, and the company will have no choice but to fund you like one.

IF YOU SOUND LIKE SUPPORT, YOU GET CUT LIKE SUPPORT

Executives make one decision fast: is this team a revenue driver, or cost center? They decide based on the words you use.

Most Account Managers accidentally teach leadership to treat them as overhead.

If all you can talk about is relationships, adoption, QBRs, and customer happiness, you sound like a cost. When budgets tighten, costs get cut.

Talk about retained revenue, expansion, and forecast accuracy? You are at the heart of the business, driving growth. Growth engines get protected.

CHAPTER 4:

VALUE BEFORE REVENUE

Imagine you are invited to present your Account Management strategy and results at the upcoming executive meeting. As you make your presentation, what do you think the CEO will be wondering about most: effort or results?

Which would they rather hear?

"We conducted 35 QBRs this quarter, updated 72 account plans, called 194 clients, and had 344 Zoom calls. We even did a team offsite in Palm Springs to 'get strategic.'"

Or:

"We had a GRR of 91% and an NRR of 108%, won back two customers from last quarter's risk list, increased deferred revenue by $11 million, and generated $17 million in expansion pipeline. All within 3% of our previous forecast."

Easy question. CEOs value results, not effort.

Great Account Managers operate with the same mindset. They create results for their customers, then make those results visible. They understand the link between value and revenue, and they know revenue comes after value.

THE DUAL MANDATE

In the last chapter, we saw why helpfulness is a dead end: you can be appreciated and still get cut. The answer isn't to stop helping. It's to change what helping means.

Your customer doesn't care about your revenue goals. They care about their goals. The Post-Sale function exists to deliver revenue, but it only lasts when customers can point to results and say, "This made a difference."

That's why the Growth Department has two inseparable jobs. First, you help your customers grow by solving meaningful problems in their business. Second, you help your company grow by delivering profitable, durable revenue back to the business. The mistake is treating those jobs as separate, yet most teams were never built to hold both.

> **Customer improvement without revenue is charity. Revenue without customer improvement is extraction.**

When customers get measurable results, revenue follows. The problem is that most teams get stuck right here. You're told to "create and show value," but no one teaches you how to define it, measure it, or make it visible in a way that customers can defend internally. Figuring this out is one of the highest points of leverage you have.

Jim Richmond is the Chief Customer Officer at Smartling, an AI translation and localization company. He wants to "upend the traditional QBR motion" so it stops being about what your team did and becomes about what the customer was able to do with your help.

That matters because the baseline rises fast. Yesterday's win becomes today's expectation, and if you're not intentional about making customers aware of the progress they've made, they'll stop noticing it. The work doesn't become less valuable. It just becomes less legible.

Richmond is careful about how you show value. "I want to remind them of the great things that they were able to do while I was holding their coat," he told me. Your job isn't to make yourself the hero of the account. It's to make the customer the hero inside their own organization, then give them the evidence to prove it.

This also solves the "define value" problem. If you ask a customer, "What does value mean to you?" you often get vague answers, because you're asking them to invent the definition from scratch. Richmond's approach is to walk in with a point of view, then invite the customer to refine it. Start with a hypothesis: "Here's how we think about value," then ask, "Does this feel right to you?" Customers engage faster when they're correcting and sharpening than when they're staring at a blank page.

Richmond jokes that your posture shouldn't be Luke Skywalker. It should be Obi-Wan or Yoda. Being customer-centric doesn't mean you do whatever the customer says. It means you bring expertise, perspective, and judgment to help them reach a better outcome than they'd reach on their own.

Make the customer the hero. Be the guide who makes progress measurable and impossible to ignore.

Define it. Measure it. Keep it in their line of sight. You stop hoping renewals happen and start earning them. The customer isn't buying your responsiveness. They're buying outcomes they can defend in a budget meeting.

WHAT DRIVES EXPANSION

Brent Adamson co-authored *The Challenger Sale*, one of the most widely read books in B2B sales. His latest book, *The Framemaking Sale*, extends that research into how customers decide to renew and expand.

When I spoke with Adamson, he described a survey his team ran with about a thousand Account Managers. They asked what works best to grow revenue with existing customers. "Eighty-eight percent believed that the single best way to drive account growth was to provide above-and-beyond service," he told me. Delight them, exceed expectations, make them so happy they want to give you more business.

But the data showed that happy customers don't spend more. They just stay.

From the customer's perspective, a renewal is a status quo decision: should we keep doing what we're doing? An expansion is a change decision: should we do something different? "Just because I'm satisfied doesn't mean I'm going to grow with you," Adamson explained.

So what actually drives expansion?

Adamson calls it Customer Improvement: "engaging your customer with an insight about their business, agnostic of yours, that helps them find new ways to make money, save money, or mitigate risk in ways they hadn't appreciated."

Your job is not to provide information, but to reduce uncertainty.

The moment you lead with their business instead of your product? You start being treated as a partner, not just another vendor.

But improvement alone isn't enough. Adamson's research surfaced a second factor that dwarfed everything else: Customer Confidence. "The single biggest driver of a high-quality, low-regret deal was the degree to which customers reported a high level of confidence in the decisions that they're making on behalf of their company," he told me. "It doesn't go up by 1x or 2x. It goes up by 10x. There's literally nothing else that comes close."

Your customers are asking themselves: Can we get our colleagues aligned? Will our organization find a way to screw this up even if the solution is right? Those barriers stall decisions, and none of them have anything to do with how good your product is.

You help customers feel confident by quantifying results instead of recapping activity, simplifying choices instead of adding options, and anticipating concerns before they surface.

Adamson tells you what makes customers expand: improvement and confidence. But what makes them stay?

MEASUREMENT DELIVERS RESULTS

If there's one person who has changed how I think about customer value, it's Greg Daines.

Daines runs ChurnRX, a firm that has built one of the largest retention datasets I've seen, with more than two million retention data points. His work has given the Post-Sale field something it has rarely had: evidence.

When I asked Daines about the connection between customer happiness and retention: "No matter where we test it, no matter how large our sample is, we always get the same result," he told me. "There's absolutely no correlation whatsoever between how happy customers say they are, using any scale, and how long they stay."

Daines experienced this firsthand when Apple was his client. "They were the worst," he said. "They complained and they were mean to us and everything was wrong." At one point he asked them directly: if you hate us so much, why don't you cancel? The response was revealing. "The guy was confused. Like, 'why would I cancel when you get us such great results?'"

That moment crystallized his point: customers don't stay because they're happy. They stay because the results work.

So if you've been optimizing for "happy" instead of "measurable," you've been playing the wrong game.

When Daines grouped customers by whether they could prove measurable outcomes, customers who achieved measurable results stayed six times longer than those who didn't.

Customers who achieved measurable results stayed six times longer.

A strange finding: even customers with poor results, if they were at least tracking them, stayed twice as long as customers who measured nothing at all. "Measurement itself creates retention," Daines explained. "Once customers can see results in their own data, they anchor to you."

He described a client in email marketing whose customers tracked a simple metric: did anyone buy something from an email they sent? The turning point for retention didn't come when customers saw impressive Return on Investment (ROI). It came when they saw their first dollar. "Nobody bought that solution to make one dollar," Daines said. "But that's when they stopped churning."

You're helping customers change how they operate so they can meet their objectives.

Most Account Managers hesitate to share bad data, worrying it will damage the relationship. Daines found the opposite. "You should absolutely show them bad data," he said. "When you show them bad data, it opens up the conversation: 'here's why.' There were five things we talked about you doing. You only did two of them." If your project is generating poor results, your customer already senses it. You earn their respect by being direct.

Daines reframes how we should think about renewals. Customers don't renew because of what you delivered last year. They already paid for that. "Renewal is a forward-looking decision," he said. "It's not enough to say, 'look what we achieved.' Renewal is 'you should do it again.'"

This is what Daines calls Customer Bonding: when a customer can no longer imagine their future success without you in it. When that bond forms, renewals stop being negotiations. "Customers who have that thing happening stay ten times longer in our data than customers who don't," he told me.

Adamson shows what drives expansion: improvement and confidence. Daines shows what drives retention: measurable results, made visible. Together, they point to the same mechanism.

THE VALUE-REVENUE CHAIN

The Value-Revenue Chain is how you make value visible and revenue predictable. It has five links: Define, Create, Measure, Show, and Earn. Each link builds on the one before it.

THE VALUE-REVENUE CHAIN

Define	Create	Measure	Show	Earn

Strengthen every link, and your revenue becomes more predictable, more profitable, and easier to defend. Weak links are where renewals turn into negotiations.

Define. The first job is to define value in the customer's terms. Not what your product does, but what the customer is trying to accomplish. Most teams rush through this step or skip it entirely. Without a proper definition, you're aiming at a moving target.

Create. Once value is defined, everything you do should connect back to it. You're not implementing software or delivering a service. You're helping the customer close the distance between where they are and where they said they want to be.

Measure. Agree on a single source of truth for the metrics that matter and track them consistently. It doesn't have to be sophisticated. A shared spreadsheet works. What matters is that both sides can see progress, or lack of it, without debating whose numbers are right.

Show. If customers don't see the value, it doesn't exist. Once an improvement becomes the new normal, people forget how bad it was before. That's why you have to keep showing the before-and-after regularly, with a clear picture of results.

Earn. When the first four links are strong, the commercial conversation gets a lot easier. You defined success, delivered results, and made it visible. Renewal becomes confirmation, not negotiation.

What does this mean on Monday morning? Before your next customer meeting, ask: which link is weak? Can they say the goal in one sentence? Can they point to a number that proves progress? If not, that's your agenda.

THE VALUE-REVENUE CHAIN IN PRACTICE

A hospital network bought a workflow automation platform to improve patient flow. Discharge times were backing up the entire system, and the COO had been fighting complaints for months.

The Account Manager helped the COO define value as reducing average discharge time from five hours to three-and-a-half within six months. That single measurable goal became the shared definition of success. Not a dashboard. Not a dozen metrics. One goal everyone could repeat.

The work meant partnering with nursing staff, case managers, and transport services to identify where handoffs were breaking down.

The team tracked discharge time weekly. By month three: four hours. By month five: three-and-a-half. Because they tracked continuously, they caught stalls early.

The Account Manager created a one-page summary showing discharge time before and after. She presented it at their quarterly review. The COO forwarded it to the hospital CEO that afternoon with a note: "This is working. Let's expand this."

The renewal conversation was short. The Account Manager opened with: "We reduced discharge time by 30%, and the COO has already asked about expanding to two more facilities. Here's what that could look like." No negotiation over price. The customer had seen the results and wanted more.

YOUR JOB IS REVENUE

I know this next part makes some people uncomfortable. It might even feel like it cuts against everything you believe about being customer-focused. Stick with me.

Your job is revenue. Not supporting revenue. Owning it.

Some people worry that owning revenue will turn them into sales-people, compromise their customer relationships, or make them less strategic. So they keep revenue at arm's length, treating it as someone else's responsibility.

That instinct is understandable. And it's the thing holding you back.

I'm not saying "become sales." I'm saying revenue is the scorecard for whether you helped the customer realize value. We have to kill this idea that revenue and customer focus are opposites. That revenue is dirty and customer focus is pure. That the best way to serve customers is to stay as far from commercial outcomes as possible.

That framing feels noble, but it keeps you small and your function underfunded.

> **Revenue is not the opposite of customer-centricity. Revenue is the proof that customer-centricity worked.**

Satisfaction matters. It's table stakes. But it's not what creates growth. Customer success is the leading indicator; revenue is the lagging indicator.

When a customer renews, they're confirming the value was real. When they expand, they're asking for more of what you delivered. Revenue isn't a betrayal of the relationship. It's the evidence that the relationship produced something worth paying for.

Being responsible for revenue doesn't mean chasing signatures or pushing for deals. It means seeing the full chain from customer outcomes to company growth and taking responsibility for both.

The Growth Department doesn't avoid revenue. It earns revenue by creating value first.

But results aren't sustainable if they depend on heroics and luck. The next chapter is about building a system that makes them repeatable.

ARE YOU PUTTING VALUE BEFORE REVENUE?

If you want to know whether you're operating as the Growth Department, ask yourself:

→ Can you define the customer's goal in one sentence?

→ Can you point to results you created, not just work you did?

→ Are you tracking value in the customer's numbers, not just in internal tools?

→ Are you showing progress regularly, not only at renewal time?

→ Can you tie each renewal or expansion to visible business outcomes?

→ Are you speaking value first, revenue second?

→ Are you treating revenue as earned, not assumed?

If a few of these aren't true yet, that's where your leverage is.

CHAPTER 5:

HOW WINNING TEAMS OPERATE

The signatures are in and the renewal contract gets logged in the CRM. It feels like you can finally declare victory, breathe for a moment, and relax.

But this renewal was a slog: it closed at 11:00 p.m. on the last day of the quarter, required three escalations, and burned through every favor you had saved up. You know there's a better way, but every quarter seems to end the same way: stress, chaos, and a win you're not sure you can repeat.

That chaos is the difference between the JV team and the Varsity team.

The JV approach treats every renewal as a unique emergency. You offer a discount to get the signature. You loop in your manager for air cover. You make promises to the customer that someone else will have to keep. It closes, and you turn to the next fire without asking why it went sideways.

The Varsity team plays a different game. Renewals close early because someone started 120 days out, with a defined sequence. Expansions land because someone spotted the opportunity before the customer asked. Forecasts are commitments, not wishes. There's no chaos because someone built a system to prevent it.

Most mature functions inside your company operate this way. Finance closes the books on a defined schedule with defined controls. Sales runs deals through stages, inspections, and forecasts that leadership can bank on. Post-Sale often doesn't get that same rigor.

When Post-Sale teams can't forecast accurately, leadership treats them like a cost center. Results that depend on heroics can't scale, and without a shared language for how the work gets done, every Account Manager reinvents the wheel.

The Growth Department operates with precision because that rigor creates freedom. It's how you stop living quarter to quarter.

SYSTEMS ARE THE DIFFERENTIATOR

Craig Rosenberg has a clear diagnosis for what holds Account Management back. "It isn't a people problem," he told me. "It's a systems problem."

Most organizations believe talent can offset the absence of structure. It can't. When there's no defined process, you resort to individual heroics and tribal knowledge. Your best Account Manager

You end up busy with work that doesn't matter, while the work that does gets pushed to nights and weekends. You exhaust yourself earning appreciation from people who don't control your results, while the outcomes you're actually measured on slip further away.

Benjamin Hardy is an organizational psychologist and the author of *10x Is Easier than 2x* and *The Science of Scaling*. His work has shaped a lot of my thinking on this topic. Hardy calls this problem "remaining below your floor."

"The floor defines what you don't do," Hardy writes. Most people focus on adding more. More activity, more effort, more hours. But real growth comes from subtraction. You have to clear out the habits, requests, and commitments that were once acceptable but now work against the results you're responsible for.

A full calendar can feel productive, but that kind of activity is performance without impact. Raising your floor starts with admitting what produces outcomes and what just fills time.

For you, this means getting ruthless about protecting customer time. It means saying no to requests that don't advance Keep, Grow, or No Surprises. It means treating your energy as the limited resource it is and investing it where the returns are real.

So do what Kane did. Color-code a week. Protect three critical hours for customer work. Treat them the way you'd treat an external meeting with your most important account. When conflicts appear, negotiate instead of surrendering.

Then pick one energy drain and eliminate it. A recurring meeting, a task, a request that doesn't advance an account. End it, shorten it, delegate it, or automate it. You don't have to fix everything at once. Start with one thing and reclaim that time for work that matters.

And once you start doing that, you run into the next problem. You have to explain the trade-offs to the people who benefit from your calendar being full.

THE UNCOMFORTABLE CONVERSATION

Raising your floor means pushing back on your boss. In cultures where being busy looks like commitment, that will create friction. But you're not asking for less work. You're asking to do the right work.

Frame it the way Alex Kane did. Don't complain about being overwhelmed. Bring the data: here's where my time is going, here's what isn't getting done, and here's the revenue at risk if I can't get upstream with these accounts. Make it about outcomes. The conversation changes. You're not protecting your calendar for comfort. You're protecting the work that produces results.

You don't get scored on internal meetings, Slack responsiveness, or a pristine CRM. You get scored on whether you helped the company win: renewals, expansions, and relationships that didn't blow up. If your calendar is full of work that never touches that scoreboard, you're optimizing for the wrong game.

Don't argue about workload. Argue about allocation. "If I spend 12 hours a week on internal asks, we lose upstream time in the accounts that renew the book."

Now zoom out. The same tax exists on the customer side, and owners reduce it.

PROTECT YOUR CUSTOMER'S ENERGY

This isn't only an internal problem. Your customers are paying a similar tax.

They have their own internal meetings, their own reporting cycles, their own requests pulling them in every direction. Every vendor they work with wants a QBR. Every project needs a status call. Every initiative requires stakeholder alignment they don't have time to build.

The Growth Department doesn't add work. It removes friction.

Solving Bigger Problems requires executive attention, and attention is scarce. Relentless Curiosity needs space to hear truth, but rushed customers give scripted answers. Acting Like an Owner means reducing friction for the business, internally and externally.

→ **Go asynchronous first.** Send a one-page update that ends with the decision you need. Something like: "Here's where we are, here's what I recommend, here's the decision we need by Thursday. If you agree, reply 'yes' and we'll execute." If you still need a meeting, it will be shorter and more focused. You don't steal their week to get your answer.

→ **Run outcome-only meetings.** Start with "Here's what changed, here's what didn't, here's the decision." End early when you get it. Turn QBRs into 25 minutes: outcomes, risks, next commitments. No slides unless they're really needed. Every meeting ends with a decision or it shouldn't have been a meeting.

→ **Remove friction**. Consolidate asks. Minimize stakeholder effort. Provide templates. Don't ask the customer to "figure out internal alignment" alone. Write the internal email for them. Bring the map, the language, and the plan. Do the work that makes it easy for them to say yes.

TRY THIS TOMORROW

Run a calendar audit on one week. Mark customer-facing work in green, everything else in red. See the ratio.

Then protect three critical hours next week. Block them for customer work. When conflicts appear, negotiate (delegate, defer, or delete) instead of surrendering.

The artifact: A weekly calendar audit. Red for internal, green for customer-facing, and a target ratio you hold yourself to.

The metric: Hours spent on customer outcomes versus internal administration.

The failure mode: Burnout. Your best people leave. The ones who stay operate in survival mode, and the method collapses under the weight of the Account Management Tax.

Now you've got the method. Next you need the structure that keeps it running. That's Part IV.

CAPACITY CREATES RESULTS

When you protect your energy, the other three Arrows become possible. You have time to prepare, to think ahead, to notice things you would have missed when you were rushing.

Net Revenue Retention doesn't compound because teams work harder. It compounds because they have the capacity to do the right work consistently. Every hour lost to the Account Management Tax is an hour you're not protecting and growing the revenue that's already yours.

Part III has given you the method: Four Arrows that point toward growth. But method alone isn't enough. It must be supported by structure: the operating rhythm, the metrics, and the organizational design that make the Growth Department real.

That's what Part IV delivers.

THE PROTECT YOUR ENERGY RULES

1. No internal meeting without a customer outcome tied to Keep, Grow, or No Surprises.

2. No recurring meeting survives without a quarterly audit. If it doesn't produce decisions, kill it.

3. No same-day responses to non-urgent internal requests. Batch them.

4. No QBR deck over 10 slides. If you can't say it in 10, you don't know what matters.

5. No "quick sync" that doesn't have an agenda and a decision to make.

6. No admin work during peak customer hours. Block 9-11am for external-facing work.

7. No CRM updates that take longer than the customer conversation they document.

8. No escalation without a proposed solution. You bring the problem and the fix.

9. No template you use more than twice stays un-templated. Systematize the repeatable.

10. No heroics that mask a broken process. If you're saving something that shouldn't need saving, surface it.

BRINGING THE AMPLIFY METHOD TO YOUR TEAM

You've just read four chapters on how to think and operate differently. You're ready to bring this to your team. Good. Here's how to make it stick.

Don't turn this into a rollout. The moment you announce a "new methodology" with a deck and a kickoff meeting, people brace for another initiative that will fade in six weeks.

Start by practicing it yourself. Pick one Arrow. If your calendar looks like Alex Kane's, color-code a week and fix one thing. If you're stuck in the vendor box with a key account, try Joanna's question: where do you want to be in five years?

Once you've felt the change, share what happened. Not as a framework, but as a story. That's how ideas spread on teams: one person tries something, gets a result, and tells the story.

When you're ready to bring it to the team, start with the Arrow that solves the most obvious problem. Meet people where the pain is. You don't need buy-in from everyone. You need one or two people willing to try something different.

Expect friction. Sales might say you're overstepping. Product might ignore you. Support might push back. That doesn't mean you're wrong. It means you're changing the rules.

The mistake is trying to win those conversations with opinions. If someone questions your priorities, bring evidence. If someone says stay in your lane, show the expansion you surfaced. You're not trying to be loud. You're trying to be undeniable.

Keep it small. Pick one account. Ask one better question. Tie the work to one outcome. Capture the result. Share it: what changed, what risk got surfaced, what surprise got avoided. People don't follow frameworks. They follow proof.

PART IV

RUNNING THE
GROWTH DEPARTMENT

CHAPTER 10:

BUILDING THE GROWTH DEPARTMENT

Michael Rapp is proof that you don't need a sales background to become a Chief Revenue Officer.

He began his career in professional services, guiding customers through implementations and seeing the issues and pressures that surface inside every account. He was inside the reality customers lived with every day, and he saw how quickly trust eroded when expectations slipped.

When he got into Account Management, Rapp already understood how customers thought and what they expected. He knew the pressure of delivering real results, not promises. The difference between new business and existing business became clear to him early. "On the new logo side, everything's all shiny and new and there's no baggage," he told me. "In Account Management, you have to deal with reality."

The turning point came when Rapp joined IntelePeer as Senior Vice President of Account Management. He went from managing around 150 accounts at his previous company to taking responsibility for more than 2,500 customers inside a 300-person company. At that scale, the install base becomes strategic. As he put it, "It's cheaper to retain and grow customers than it is to acquire new customers. When you think about a SaaS business with recurring revenue, the existing customer base and that retention are critically important."

That visibility shaped how he understood the entire revenue picture, and after three years with the company, he stepped in to support new business as well. When IntelePeer's CRO retired, Rapp became the natural successor. He had what he called "the full revenue cycle view, from selling, to growing, to keeping."

"It's not just getting the new logos," he said. "We've got to keep the revenue in the barn as well."

I like this story because it shows a real path to the CRO seat, and because it reveals what made the structure work.

For the Growth Department to succeed, the surrounding structure has to support it. You need a system that reinforces Keep, Grow, No Surprises and aligns the organization around those outcomes.

You don't need a dramatic reorganization to get there. This chapter shows you how to build that structure: how to position the Growth Department inside the revenue organization, how to connect the work to decisions across the company, and how to make leadership confident enough to invest in long-term growth.

A UNIFIED REVENUE TEAM

Rapp came up through Post-Sale. Other CROs come up through sales. The path doesn't matter. What matters is the structure. One CRO over all revenue.

The Growth Department wins by delivering profitable revenue back to the business. NRR is how you are measured and delivering it is how you help your company win.

NRR is a revenue number. Revenue numbers roll up to the CRO.

Here's where most companies get this wrong. They treat CRO like a fancy title for head of Sales. It isn't. CRO stands for Chief Revenue Officer. All revenue, not the new business slice. All of it.

The cleanest structure puts all revenue under one leader. The CRO owns the full number across the customer lifecycle: new business, renewals, and expansion. Not because Sales and Growth do the same job, but because revenue decisions need one home. When you split the number, you split decisions. When you split decisions, you lose.

This is the change most companies haven't made: the VP of Growth must report to the CRO.

Not to the CEO. Not to the COO. Not through a Chief Customer Officer who can advocate but can't decide. To the CRO. Because your job is revenue, you belong inside the revenue organization.

The whole book has been leading you here.

The AMplify Method makes you effective inside the account. This structure makes the company recognize that work as what it is: revenue. Without the structure, you're fighting for visibility. With it, you become the person everyone turns to when revenue needs to be understood.

Two leaders report to the CRO: VP Sales and VP Growth. Together, they own the entire revenue picture without overlap or confusion.

The lines stay clear. Sales finds opportunities, runs the deal, and brings new customers into the business. Growth owns everything that follows. Guiding the relationship, helping customers reach meaningful outcomes, and delivering the revenue tied to retention and expansion. Keep, Grow, No Surprises.

This separation protects what makes each role work. Sales thrives on the hunt and the close; Growth thrives on long-term thinking, multi-threaded relationships, and helping customers make smart internal decisions. These are different jobs with distinct rhythms. If you try to blend them, you weaken both.

If you own NRR, you're the VP of Growth, whatever your title says today.

Who owns existing-customer revenue in your company right now? If the answer isn't one person inside the revenue organization, you've found the problem. Now you know exactly how to fix it.

PEOPLE WILL PUSH BACK

This isn't about diminishing the customer voice. It's about giving that voice real authority, the kind that comes with owning a number.

When you try to implement this model, you will meet resistance.

"Growth should report to the CEO or COO."

This usually sounds like: "Customer experience is too important to sit inside the revenue org. It needs a direct line to the top."

The moment Growth reports outside the revenue organization, it gets separated from the decisions that shape revenue. The CRO makes calls about forecasting, pipeline tradeoffs, and investment allocation. If Growth isn't in that conversation, the customer base becomes an afterthought. Investment decisions favor acquisition by default. When Growth sits outside revenue, NRR becomes an influence goal instead of an owned number.

If you want customers represented at the top, give Growth a seat inside revenue, not outside it.

"We need a Chief Customer Officer."

This usually sounds like: "We need someone at the table whose only job is advocating for customers."

In Chapter 1, we named this problem. A customer leader with relationship responsibility but no revenue authority becomes a ceremonial title. They can advocate, but they can't decide. When budget gets allocated and tradeoffs get made, the person without a number loses. They end up explaining churn instead of preventing it.

NRR is a revenue number. The person who owns it needs to sit inside the revenue organization, with the authority to make revenue decisions. That's not advocacy. That's accountability.

Call it CCO if you want. But give them the NRR number and have them report to the CRO. At that point, you've built exactly what this chapter describes: a VP of Growth with a fancier title.

"The CRO should focus on new business."

This usually sounds like: "The CRO is really the head of Sales. Customer retention is a different discipline."

If the CRO only owns new business, they own the minority of the number. The person who owns the base becomes the real revenue leader. Accountability for NRR disappears, and when the board asks why retention is slipping, nobody in the revenue organization can answer.

EXPECT THE OLD PLAYBOOK TO DEFEND ITSELF

The Old Playbook will resist replacement. People who built careers on relationship management without commercial accountability will feel threatened, Sales leaders who've owned "revenue" as a title will push back on sharing it, and executives who've never had to forecast the base will resist being held to a number.

That resistance isn't a sign you're wrong. It's a sign you're changing something that needed changing.

You can't win these battles with opinions. You win them with evidence. Show the NRR trend. Show the surprise churn. Show the expansion left on the table. The Old Playbook holds up until someone does the math.

HOW GROWTH CONNECTS THE COMPANY

Dave Jackson has spent three decades in customer leadership and is the author of *Customer-Led Growth*. He told me the biggest barrier to delivering successful customers isn't talent or tools. It's the organization itself. "We keep rearranging the boxes on the org chart," he said, "instead of building the connective tissue that joins up Marketing, Sales, Product, and Post-Sale."

The Growth Department sits at the center of the customer experience, so it connects the work of every team that touches revenue.

Because the Growth Department sits at the center of the customer reality, it acts as that connective tissue. But this isn't about "collaboration" or "staying aligned." It's about intel. You possess the data that other departments are starving for.

Growth Feeds Marketing: Marketing teams often guess at what messaging works. You know what converts. When you share the exact words customers use to describe value, marketing stops writing fluff and starts writing copy that sells.

Growth Feeds Product: Product teams drown in feature requests. You see the difference between what customers ask for and what they adopt. When you share data on where customers get stuck, you help Product stop building "nice-to-haves" and start fixing the friction that kills NRR.

Growth Feeds Finance: Finance hates surprises. A forecast based on "sentiment" is a liability; a forecast based on engagement data is an asset. When you provide an early view of risk and expansion, you give the CFO the confidence to allocate capital.

Growth Feeds Sales: Sales teams need social proof. You own the referenceable customers. When Growth and Sales align, the "ideal customer profile" stops being a theory and becomes a mirror of your most successful accounts.

But if Growth is going to change decisions across the company, it has to be funded like a revenue function.

THE LANGUAGE THAT CHANGES BUDGETS

Rav Dhaliwal, a venture capital investor and former executive at Zendesk and Slack, summed up the Post-Sale mission in two sentences:

"The reason we have Customer Success and Account Management is we want to deliver on the value we promised when we sold. We want to help customers realize value quickly, with minimal effort, so we have a wide window to do more business with them."

That's the blueprint for the Growth Department. Our job is to accelerate value so customers can expand. When customers see measurable results early, the door to future growth stays open. The longer it takes them to reach value, the smaller that door becomes.

Accelerating value realization is the most reliable lever you have to drive both Gross and Net Revenue Retention.

Dhaliwal explained that many teams forget this foundation. "The reason we exist is to accelerate value so we can sell them more.

Somewhere along the way, that got lost." Too often, Customer Success and Account Management get buried in internal tasks and lose sight of the larger commercial goal.

Dhaliwal thinks job titles matter more than people admit. "I would retire the name Customer Success. If I were founding a company today, I'd have Sales and Growth. The Growth team would own adoption, feature consumption, and revenue expansion."

And when it comes to getting budget: "Budget proposals framed as growth headcount attract more support than requests for success resources."

Walk into a budget meeting asking for "Customer Success headcount," and you're asking for a cost. Walk in asking for "Growth capacity," and you're asking for an investment. Same people, same work, different answer.

Now you know where the Growth Department belongs and how to talk about it. The next question is how to run it.

Chapter 11 gives you the operating system: the portfolio model that focuses attention, the risk discipline that surfaces problems early, and the cadence that ties it all together.

THE ORG CHART STRESS TEST

You can't execute a growth strategy with a support structure. If your org chart is fighting your revenue goals, the org chart will win.

Use these four tests to see whether your design is helping or blocking growth.

The Unity Test: Does one leader own the entire revenue number, both new business and existing business? Or is ownership split across Sales, Success, and Operations?

The Focus Test: Are you asking the same role to drive adoption and negotiate renewals or expansions? If yes, you're creating incentive conflict and mediocre performance in both.

The Voice Test: Does the leader who owns the customer base have an equal seat at the executive table? Or is their influence limited by title or reporting line?

The Flow Test: Does customer insight reach Product and Marketing directly? Or does it die in decks, dashboards, and QBR notes that no one reads?

If you failed one of these tests, your people aren't the problem. It's the design.

CHAPTER 11:

THE GROWTH OPERATING SYSTEM

When I asked Justin Strackany what he would say to a burned-out Account Manager staring at an overloaded book of business, he didn't hesitate:

"Slow down, take a breath," he said. "Some accounts will spend money now. Some will grow over time. Everyone else belongs in the third bucket. Find the 20% that matter. Focus on them."

Strackany earned that view over 18 years at SecureLink. He joined as employee number one, managed key accounts, led the team, ran Sales, and eventually became Chief Customer Officer. He owned the results of the entire customer base through multiple exits.

At one point, he ran his team on a rule that would alarm most organizations: "We paid our Account Managers off of straight NRR percentage. If you lost an $80,000 account that month, you had some work to do. You needed 100% NRR to keep your job."

That wasn't cruel. It was clear.

"Customer Success is about revenue," he told me. "It has always been. It's time to let go of the idea that we can sit to the side and let the grownups talk about money. We are supposed to be the grownups."

Strackany saw the fundamental disconnect in most Post-Sale teams. The expectations had expanded to include commercial ownership, but the systems around them remained anchored in reactive support. The expectations had evolved. The operating model had not.

So he stopped managing relationships and started managing a portfolio. When the system's broken, more effort doesn't fix it. The answer is to operate like someone who owns a financial asset.

"Build workflows around the core activities," he said. "Automate the mechanics so your attention goes where it matters."

Strackany was running a Growth Department before the language existed. NRR was the scoreboard. If a major customer slipped, you didn't spin a narrative. You fixed the portfolio.

When the system works, you no longer need the heroics.

Strackany didn't fix churn with hustle. He fixed it with a system. That system starts with a simple decision: where does your best attention actually go?

SEGMENTATION AND COVERAGE

In Chapter 2, we talked about why portfolios matter. A portfolio isn't a collection of relationships. It's an asset you're trying to grow. And in any portfolio, some holdings will underperform. Some will leave. That's normal.

The Growth Department doesn't pretend churn never happens. You've got to protect the base, but the bigger job is to find the customers with the highest probability of expansion and orient the team around them. That's how portfolios grow: you put your best attention where the upside is, and you stop spending premium effort on accounts that can't realistically compound.

Segmentation is one of the best tools you have for doing that well.

Segmentation is the act of deciding, on purpose, where value and risk actually live. Which customers justify your highest-touch work? Which ones can grow with the right plays? Which ones should run on automation until something changes? Which ones are quietly at risk even though they feel fine?

There's no universal model. Your segmentation will vary based on company size, pricing model, industry, average contract value, gross margin, product complexity, sales cycle, implementation effort, and the maturity of your team. A $20M company and a $500M company shouldn't segment the same way. A tech company selling to small businesses and an enterprise services company shouldn't segment the same way. Even two companies with the same revenue can need radically different approaches.

Segmentation determines who gets a named owner, how often you meet, when you escalate, and where you add headcount. If you skip it and jump straight to coverage models, you're just guessing with more steps.

Segmentation tells the team where to focus. Without it, every account feels equally urgent; with it, you can finally treat the base like the portfolio it is.

If you're stuck on segmentation, start simple. Plot your accounts on two axes: current revenue (vertical) and expansion potential (horizontal). The top-right quadrant gets your best attention. The bottom-left gets automation.

The next job is making sure bad news shows up early enough to do something about it.

NO SURPRISES IS A DISCIPLINE

When churn is obvious, you're already late. I've sat in enough post-mortems to know: the warning signs were there months earlier. Someone wasn't paying attention. If you wait for obvious symptoms, you're not managing risk. You're reacting to it.

Nothing damages credibility faster than bad news that came without warning.

At Asana, Josh Abdulla's answer is the Red Renewals Program, which flags at-risk enterprise accounts nine to twelve months before renewal. Most teams wait until 90 days out. That's too late. "Your churn this quarter is basically baked," he told me. "You might impact churn a quarter out, definitely two quarters out, absolutely three and four quarters out. So you have to find problems early enough to actually fix them."

Red means the renewal outcome is in doubt. Yellow means it can still go either way. But color isn't the point. Ownership is. Risk needs a home, not scattered across inboxes and memory. A risk register gives it that home: the account and revenue at stake, what you're seeing, who owns the response, what happens next, and what triggers escalation.

Signals are tracked systematically. Product utilization is one trigger: "If fewer than 70% of users log in within a 90-day window, that's a risk to us," Abdulla explained. Support ticket patterns surface friction. Qualitative factors matter too: champion departures, executive turnover, competitive pressure. Not all signals are equal. "Product utilization being low is a symptom, not a cause in most cases," he said. Leading indicators take more effort to track, but they buy you time. Did your sponsor leave? Is procurement suddenly involved? Are competitors being mentioned?

Every two weeks, Abdulla's leadership team reviews new red renewals with the CSMs who own them: what's going on, when did you last talk to the customer, when was the last QBR or onsite? The questions are consistent. The goal is to coach, not catch.

Michael Rapp runs a similar discipline at IntelePeer. When an account goes red, the Account Manager produces a "get to green" plan: concrete actions to stabilize the account, grounded in what they're hearing from the customer, not only what the dashboard says.

When an account goes red, the worst thing you can do is let it stay vague. Within 72 hours you should be able to answer three questions: who owns recovery, what happens next, and when do we escalate?

When Abdulla arrived at Asana, surprise churns were common. "My first quarter, we were surprised by some very, very large churns that we just weren't forecasting, we weren't on top of," he said. Within a year, that changed. "Now I'm proud to say there are no surprises. We know them, we're ahead of them, we know how to engage our execs with the customer."

A risk register is useless if it isn't reviewed. The difference between "we track risk" and "we prevent surprises" is rhythm.

THE RHYTHM THAT REPLACES HEROICS

The Growth Department runs on three cycles. If you're not making decisions, it's status reporting.

The weekly meeting is where you keep promises. Keep it short and brutally practical: red and yellow accounts only, the risk register open, and owners leaving with next actions. This isn't a strategy session. **The monthly meeting** is where you identify issues before they become churn. Step back from immediate renewals and look at the full portfolio. Segment distribution, GRR and NRR trends, red/yellow/green across the base. What's changing, what's stuck, where are you under-covered?

The quarterly meeting is where the base meets the business. CRO, VP of Growth, and whoever else needs to be there. Not a standing committee, but the people who can really make decisions. Cohort analysis showing which segments retain and expand, capacity planning, strategic risks, and forecast accuracy trends. The output is resource allocation: where to invest, what to fix, what to stop.

Segmentation without risk discipline still creates surprises. Rhythm without segmentation buries your best people.

When the CRO asks how the customer base is performing, you don't scramble to build a deck. You pull from data you review every week.

Start here: pick your three highest-risk renewals in the next 90 days. For each one, write down the signal that would tell you something changed. Then decide who checks for that signal and when.

AI AND WHAT REMAINS

I haven't spent much time in this book on AI, and that's intentional. Tools change. The economic reality doesn't.

But AI does create urgency for this work, because it exposes the difference between activity and value.

If your primary contribution is being responsive (answering emails quickly, pulling reports, fielding basic questions) that work is already being commoditized. AI can do it faster and cheaper.

But AI can't build trust or navigate politics inside a customer's organization. It can't look a CFO in the eye and give them the confidence to sign a $2 million renewal. And it can't ask the question that reveals a problem they didn't know they had.

That's the work of the Growth Department. Strategic, relational, human.

AI is going to compress the value of basic responsiveness fast. The teams that thrive will use it to clear the maintenance work and redirect capacity to the judgment calls that compound: trust, risk assessment, strategic conversation. If you use AI to clear admin work, you get more time for judgment, trust, and risk calls. That's where the returns are.

WHEN YOU MEET RESISTANCE

When you start operating as the Growth Department, you'll encounter friction. Sales might tell you to stay in your lane. Product might ignore your feedback. Support might resent your push for faster resolution.

Don't argue philosophy. Bring facts.

When Sales pushes back, show the expansion data: "I uncovered a $50,000 opportunity in this account by asking about their 2025 goals. Who should I hand this to?" When Product ignores you, show the revenue at risk. When Leadership questions your priorities, anchor it to NRR.

When you anchor every conversation in customer reality and revenue, you become hard to argue with.

Strackany said we're supposed to be the grownups. Grownups bring facts. They speak the language of the business. They earn their seat by making the work legible to the people who run the company.

THE SEAT YOU ALREADY OCCUPY

Joanna Hagelberger asked "Where do you want to be in five years?" and turned a $50,000 account into $10 million. Amanda Edington saved an account by listening instead of defending. Anthony De-Shazor built value so visible that contracts became unnecessary. Alex Kane color-coded her calendar and changed the structure of her team.

The Four Arrows pointing toward durable revenue. A structure that gives them a home. And now a system that makes them repeatable.

Strackany didn't wait for permission to run his team like a Growth Department. He saw the commercial reality and operated accordingly. "Customer Success is about revenue," he said. "We are supposed to be the grownups."

You stop being invisible when you run the portfolio like revenue.

You don't need a new title or a new org chart. You need the operating system.

Keep. Grow. No Surprises.

Your customers are waiting.

THE GROWTH DEPARTMENT COMMITMENT

This is what we believe.

→ Existing customers are not a cost center. They are the engine.

→ Our job is to Keep, Grow, No Surprises. Everything else is noise.

→ We don't wait for problems to surface. We see them early and act before they compound.

→ We define value with the customer, then we make it measurable.

→ We don't apologize for talking about revenue. Revenue is how we measure whether we've actually helped.

→ We protect our energy for the work that matters.

→ We own the outcome.

THE 90-DAY GROWTH DEPARTMENT INSTALL PLAN

This plan assumes you're ready to abandon the Old Playbook. If you're still debating whether the Growth Department model applies to you, go back to Part I. The economics are settled. This section is for leaders who want to implement what you just learned.

Weeks 1–2: Establish the Scorecard

→ Name the Growth owner - one person accountable for the base

→ Baseline your current NRR (calculate if you haven't) - this is your north star

→ Tier your portfolio: which accounts are stable, which have growth potential, which need a managed exit

→ Define what "red, yellow, green" means for account health

Weeks 3–6: Build the Risk System

→ Implement a risk register - every account with a flag gets documented

→ Define renewal horizon - how far out do you start active renewal management?

→ Install early warning triggers - what signals risk before the customer says it?

→ Run your first portfolio review with the leadership team

Weeks 7–10: Run the Cadence

→ Launch weekly or biweekly pipeline and risk review

→ Calibrate tier definitions based on real data

→ Adjust coverage model - who owns what, and is it sustainable?

→ Identify handoff friction between Sales, Onboarding, and Growth

Weeks 11–13: Lock the Structure

→ Align compensation to NRR outcomes, not just activity

→ Clarify role boundaries - what Growth owns, influences, and refuses

→ Formalize forecast ownership - Growth owns the existing-customer number

→ Present the 90-day results to leadership with a forward plan

YOU'RE IN THE DRIVER'S SEAT

It's easy to look at Joanna Hagelberger's results and call it luck. A customer has an urgent problem, your product fits, and the revenue line takes off.

But here's what I didn't tell you earlier. Joanna's done this more than once.

In addition to taking one customer from $50,000 to $10 million, she took another from $200,000 to $5 million. That's a 25X increase. Two different companies, two different situations, same kind of outsized growth. She didn't get lucky twice. She ran a system.

Across both accounts, you can see the Four Arrows working together: bigger problems, relentless curiosity, ownership, protected energy. That's the method. It started with a single question: where do you want to be in five years?

UNSUNG HERO NO MORE

You're here to help your company win. Durable revenue is the engine. Keep, Grow, No Surprises. That's the work. You're in the middle of it.

And you've been doing it with a fraction of the budget Sales gets and none of the recognition. That's the Account Management Tax. You don't have to keep paying it.

The unsung hero story ends when the work becomes visible. Run Post-Sale like a portfolio with a scoreboard and a cadence, and leadership starts treating it like the asset it is.

YOU'RE AT THE HEART OF THE BUSINESS

In the introduction, I told you what was missing: an operating system. Now you have one.

A scoreboard that shows you who's winning. A portfolio model that protects your most productive time. A risk discipline that surfaces problems before they become surprises. A playbook built on Keep, Grow, No Surprises. Cadences that make it repeatable.

Use that operating system and you make the work visible, teachable, and worth funding. Revenue becomes durable.

Once you see the role clearly, your options open fast. The customer base is the most durable revenue in the company. People who can run it become hard to replace.

Rapp went from Post-Sale leadership to CRO because he understood the full revenue picture. Strackany ran the base through multiple exits and treated it like an asset the whole time. Joanna built partnerships worth over $100 million in lifetime value.

Some of you will become VP of Growth. Others will become CRO or CCO. Some will build a career as the person who can take any portfolio, install a cadence, and make NRR predictable. There's no single path. The common thread is ownership.

START ANYWAY

The Old Playbook will keep running until someone replaces it. That someone is you.

Not because you have permission, but because you can see what leadership can't. The revenue is already in the building, and too few teams run it like the asset it is.

The Growth Department isn't something you request. It's something you decide to run.

You're going back to a company that may not see you the way this book does. Not yet. That's fine. Start anyway.

Pick one account that matters and get the conversation upstream. Ask a question that forces a longer horizon. Protect one hour for customer work before your calendar fills with internal noise. Put it on the calendar and keep it. Surface one risk early. Not when renewal is close, now. Make it visible. Give it an owner. Put a next step on it.

Run the 90-day install plan exactly as written. If you need a clean definition of the function, use Appendix A. If you need the executive language, use Appendix B.

Small steps, done consistently. This is how revenue compounds.

There's no such thing as recurring revenue. There's only revenue you re-earn. Every day, every account, every quarter.

Stop waiting to be recognized. Make the work impossible to ignore. The Growth Department is real. Time to act like it.

THE GROWTH DEPARTMENT CHARTER

The executive-ready definition

Definition

The Growth Department is the function responsible for existing-customer revenue: renewals, expansion, and the predictability that lets leadership plan with confidence. It is not a rebrand of Customer Success or Account Management. It is a strategic discipline with defined ownership, a clear scoreboard, and explicit boundaries.

Scope

The Growth Department owns the customer relationship from handoff through renewal and expansion. It does not own onboarding delivery (though it monitors outcomes). It does not own product adoption metrics (though it uses them as signals). It owns the revenue outcome and the forecast accuracy that proves the system works.

Scoreboard

→ Net Revenue Retention (primary)

→ Gross Revenue Retention

→ Expansion pipeline and conversion

→ Renewal rate by tier

→ Forecast accuracy (within 5%)

→ Risk coverage (% of portfolio with current health assessment)

Governance

→ Weekly: At-risk renewals in the 90-day window

→ Monthly: Full portfolio review (red/yellow/green distribution, NRR trend)

→ Quarterly: Executive growth review (cohort performance, capacity planning, strategic decisions)

Interfaces

→ **Sales:** Owns handoff quality, customer profile, expansion handoffs on new divisions

→ **Onboarding/Implementation:** Owns time-to-value; Growth monitors and escalates

→ **Product:** Growth provides revenue-weighted customer evidence; Product owns roadmap

→ **Support:** Owns ticket resolution; Growth owns relationship and commercial outcome

→ **Finance:** Growth owns forecast; Finance owns reporting and board narrative

Owns

→ Retention, expansion, and renewals

→ Net Revenue Retention as the primary scorecard

→ Renewal outcomes and expansion pipeline

→ Risk visibility across the portfolio

→ Forecast accuracy for existing accounts

→ Quality of hand-back to sales for new project opportunities

Influences

→ Product priorities through revenue impact and customer evidence

→ Marketing messaging through value proof and customer language

→ Sales enablement through customer mapping and handoff quality

→ Service delivery through customer expectations and success criteria

Refuses to Own

→ Reactive support tickets disguised as "relationship management"

→ Unlimited customization requests that erode margins

→ Surprise escalations caused by upstream neglect

→ Outcomes for customers who were mis-sold or never should have signed

The Growth Department is not a catch-all. It is a revenue function with defined accountability. When the boundaries blur, so does the budget. When accountability is clear, investment follows.

THE INTERNAL PITCH KIT

How to make the case inside your company

The 60-Second Pitch

"We manage a majority of the company's revenue with very little investment. Our best people are burning out, our forecasts are unstable, and we're losing accounts we should have saved. I want to propose a different model: one owner for existing-customer revenue, a clear scoreboard, and an operating cadence that makes risk visible before it becomes a surprise. The companies doing this are seeing double-digit improvements in Net Revenue Retention. I'd like 90 days to install the basics and show you the results."

The One-Page Memo (Outline)

1. **The problem:** Post-Sale revenue has no named owner. Forecasts are unstable. Churn surprises leadership. Best people leave.

2. **The cost:** [Insert your numbers: churned revenue, missed expansion, replacement cost, team turnover]

3. **The fix:** The Growth Department model. One owner. Clear boundaries. Portfolio tiering. Risk system. Weekly/monthly/quarterly cadence.

4. **The ask:** 90 days to install. Name an owner, baseline NRR, tier the portfolio, launch the cadence.

5. **The proof point:** [Reference Rapp at IntelePeer, or Abdulla at Asana, or your own internal evidence]

The Board Language (Why Now)

For CFOs and CEOs, frame the case in terms they already track:

→ **Risk:** "We have $X million in renewals over the next 12 months with no systematic risk visibility."

→ **Predictability:** "Our renewal forecast has been off by more than 10% in three of the last four quarters."

→ **Margin:** "Expansion revenue converts at 4x the efficiency of new business. We're underinvesting in the highest-margin path to growth."

→ **Enterprise value:** "Every point of NRR improvement increases valuation by 12-18% over five years. We're leaving value on the table."

Don't ask for permission, just make the cost of inaction obvious and the path forward clear.

Common Objections (and How to Answer Them)

Objection	Response
"We already have Customer Success."	Customer Success is a team. The Growth Department is an operating model. You can have CS people and still lack forecast ownership, risk governance, and commercial authority. This gives them the structure to drive NRR.
"This is just Account Management with a new name."	Account Management is a role. The Growth Department is a function with a defined scope, a scoreboard (NRR), and clear interfaces with Sales, Product, and Finance. The name isn't the point. The operating system is.
"Sales owns revenue."	Sales owns new revenue. Who owns the 70-80% that's already in the building? If your answer is "no one specifically," that's the problem this solves.
"We can't add headcount right now."	This isn't a headcount request. It's a structure request. You already have people doing this work. The question is whether they have the authority, the scoreboard, and the cadence to do it predictably.
"Forecasting existing customers is impossible."	It's only impossible without a system. Companies like Asana forecast churn within 3% using early warning signals, risk registers, and defined escalation paths. The system makes it possible.
"Our CRO came up through Sales and won't adopt this."	CROs who came up through Sales still own the full number. When NRR drops, they answer for it. This gives them a structure to manage the part of revenue they currently can't see.

Objection	Response
"This creates a turf war with Sales."	The boundaries are clean: Sales finds opportunities and closes new business. Growth owns everything after signature. The turf war happens when no one owns the base. This ends it.
"We're not a SaaS company, so this doesn't apply."	The economics apply anywhere customers renew or expand: professional services, logistics, healthcare, manufacturing. If you have existing-customer revenue, you have a Growth Department problem.

NOTES

Most of the quotes in this book are from my podcast, *Account Management Secrets*. For full details and to access the archive, visit https://amplifyam.com/podcast

Chapter 1

Forrester reports that 73% of B2B revenues come from existing customers, including renewals, cross-sell, and upsell, based on Forrester's Marketing Survey, 2024. (https://www.forrester.com/blogs/b2b-marketing-leaders-dont-trust-their-measurement-and-what-they-measure-isnt-helping)

Gartner data and quotes come from a survey of 243 CSOs and senior sales leaders (https://www.businesswire.com/news/home/20250520293913/en/Gartner-Survey-Finds-73-of-CSOs-Are-Prioritizing-Growth-from-Existing-Customers-for-2025)

Arthur Jones quote as cited in *Designing Organizations for High Performance* by David Hanna (Addison-Wesley, 1988).

Chapter 2

Data on Payback periods comes from The KeyBanc Capital Markets SaaS Survey, in partnership with Sapphire Ventures. (https://www.key.com/businesses-institutions/industry-expertise/library-saas-resources.html)

Expansion stats come from Ebsta's *2025 Go-to-Market (GTM) Benchmarks Report*, produced with Pavilion (https://benchmarks.ebsta.com/2025-gtm-benchmarks)

Data on Research that each one-point lift in NRR increases enterprise value by 12-18% over five years comes from m3ter and SaaS Capital (https://www.m3ter.com/blog/the-impact-of-net-revenue-retention-on-saas-company-valuations)

Data on NRR and valuation multiples comes from the Software Equity Group (SEG) SaaS Index (https://softwareequity.com/blog/net-retention-public-saas-companies/)

CAC upsell data comes from RJMetrics / Insivia (https://www.insivia.com/quoter/the-median-customer-acquisition-cost-cac-for-upsells-is-just-0-28-per-1-less-than-a-quarter-of-the-1-18-spent-to-acquire-1-of-revenue-from-a-new-customer/)

Data on renewals cost comes from 2015 Pacific Crest SaaS CEO Survey via Gainsight (https://www.gainsight.com/blog/8-customer-success-takeaways-from-the-2015-pacific-crest-saas-ceo-survey/)

Net Promoter Score® and NPS® are registered trademarks of Bain & Company, Fred Reichheld, and Satmetrix.

Chapter 3

Descriptions of Fred Kofman's work are drawn from *The Meaning Revolution* (Ebury Publishing, 2018).

Descriptions of Chad Horenfeldt's work are drawn from *The Strategic Customer Success Manager* (2024).

Data on sales performance from Ebsta's 2025 *GTM Digest: Sales Efficiency Expansion* report

Chapter 4

Descriptions of Brent Adamson's work are drawn from *The Framemaking Sale* (PublicAffairs, 2025), *The Challenger Customer* (Portfolio, 2015) and *The Challenger Sale* (Portfolio, 2011).

Chapter 9

The 10x framework comes from Dan Sullivan (Strategic Coach) and is expanded in *10x Is Easier than 2x*, co-authored with Benjamin Hardy.

Descriptions and quotes from Benjamin Hardy's work are drawn from *The Science of Scaling* (Hay House Business, 2025).

ACKNOWLEDGEMENTS

Writing *The Growth Department* was more fun, and more rewarding, than I expected. I'm grateful to the people who helped bring it to life.

Joanna Hagelberger, for trusting me with her 200x story. Megan Close Zavala, for thoughtful editing and guidance. Karolina Kruk-Umięcka, for cover and interior design. Agustin Miranda, for helping us navigate the mechanics of publishing.

Emily Main, for the research support. Jennifer Pinter, for being a constant Account Management thought partner.

Thank you to every *Account Management Secrets* podcast guest, especially those featured in this book.

Thank you to the beta readers who gave early feedback and made the manuscript sharper.

Thank you to the AMplify members who pushed my thinking and inspired this project.

And to my family: my dad, Larry Raymond, for wordsmithing help and for pushing me to put my best work on the page. My wife, Laura Guerra Raymond, for her steady encouragement and support.

ABOUT THE AUTHOR

Alex Raymond is the founder of AMplify and the host of the *Account Management Secrets* podcast. Over the past decade, he has worked with Account Managers and Post-Sale leaders to strengthen customer relationships, drive expansion, and improve renewal execution.

Alex earned a bachelor's degree from Georgetown University and an MBA from INSEAD. He lives in Boulder, Colorado, with his wife, Laura, and their dogs. *The Growth Department* is his first book.

For information about programs and workshops, or to book Alex Raymond as a keynote speaker, visit www.amplifyam.com or email tdg@amplifyam.com